Postcards
from the Garden of
Estrogen

Don Staffin

First published by Dog Ear Publishing
4010 W. 86th Street, Ste H
Indianapolis, IN 46268
www.dogearpublishing.net

ISBN: 978-160844-002-3

This book is printed on acid-free paper.

Printed in the United States of America

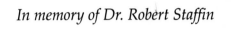

In memory of Dr. Robert Staffin

TABLE OF CONTENTS

Introduction

Prologue

In the beginning there was a boy. He had a brother, a sister, and two wonderful parents. The boy spent every possible moment with his younger brother and male friends, competing at sports, playing with toy soldiers, breaking things, etc.

The boy became a young man and attended a university. When he wasn't studying engineering, he did lots of male stuff: joined a fraternity, drank beer, played ice hockey at crazy hours of the night, etc... and then met the woman of his dreams.

The couple married and had four daughters – three at once, as a matter of fact. The kids were easy to figure out at first: eat, sleep, change diapers. However, somewhere along the way they started to grow. And as they grew, the man realized that if he had paid more attention to his sister as a child, he might have picked up a few important lessons that could have proved useful when living with five females.

Welcome to the Garden of Estrogen

Dear Reader,

Greetings, and welcome to The Garden of Estrogen. You may be prompted to ask, "What is this place?" Is it an environment where the foolish male is adrift in a sea of self pity, never able to do anything right? No (although occasionally it might seem that way). Rather, the Garden is an oasis where one can observe and learn how females look at the world – filtered through a man's eyes, of course.

For example…

The Scene: Husband and wife are standing in the kitchen putting the finishing touches on preparations for a family party that afternoon.

Wife: "What kind of wine should we serve - white or red?"

Truth be told, I'm more of a beer kind of guy, but I venture an opinion nevertheless…

Husband: "Red, I guess."

Wife: "On our white carpet? With kids around? Are you nuts?"

Husband: "If there was only one correct answer, why ask in the first place?"

Wife *(laughing)*: "I have no idea."

Does anyone else find this just a little perplexing?

* * *

A few years ago, I began to organize my observations into words, and sent my first "Postcard from the Garden of Estrogen" to about two dozen people. The response was so encouraging, I sent another – and another, etc. Before long, I started getting requests from people who had seen the Postcards and wanted to be added to the list of recipients. The list has grown steadily over the years – both inside and outside the USA.

What I have found along the way is that the Postcards generate different responses from the two sexes. Men tend to be amused by the observations and anecdotes and will often share their stories of a similar nature.

What I did not expect was that <u>women</u> would have such an overwhelmingly positive reaction. I think the reason for this is... actually, I have no idea why this is the case.

In the past few years I have been asked many times, "When is the book coming out?" This is my response. I hope you will enjoy the journey.

Don Staffin, a.k.a. "The Gardener"

Cast of Characters

I am pleased to introduce the cast of characters in the Garden of Estrogen:

The Gardener (a.k.a Father): That would be yours truly. Over the chapters that follow, it will be my distinct pleasure to guide you through the wonder and bewilderment of life with five females. An engineer by training, by day I am a business executive in supply chain management and electronic commerce in the marine industry. In my spare time I am a long distance runner, youth travel soccer coach, and writer.

The Queen (a.k.a Mother): My beloved wife. A former high school science teacher and subsequent consumer products marketing manager, The Queen has been a full-time mom since the birth of our triplets. When time permits, she conducts seminars on various topics for parents and childcare providers. She has also been the primary editor of my Postcards.

D1 (Daughter #1): The "oldest" of our triplets. She is the most circumspect of our four daughters, and the quickest wit. D1 wants to be a dairy farmer when she grows up.

D2: The "middle" triplet. The smallest of the three, D2 lives and breathes sports. She is an accomplished soccer goalie and distance runner. Her favorite letters are ESPN. At night, D2 can frequently be found sleeping in her New York Mets #5 David Wright jersey.

D3: The "youngest" triplet. She can frequently be found curled up with a book, but her gentle, mother-hen demeanor can be deceiving. She is the tallest and by far the strongest of the three, and when pressed on the athletic field or on the playground, can dish it out as well as take it.

In a previous generation, these three would be considered tomboys. All three ski, play basketball, and play competitive travel soccer. All three love music and play brass instruments. They also love animals, especially cows. They dress up nicely when the occasion requires, and they usually leave the house looking presentable. However, at least through their preteen years, they have tended to steer clear of what they consider to be "girly-girl stuff." This includes makeup, Abercrombie & Fitch clothing, and cell phone text messages. They recognize that boys are in their future, but they are in no rush to get there (which makes me very happy).

D4: Three years junior to the triplets, D4 is our socialite. She loves to dance and dress up "girly girl," according to her sisters. She has followed in their footsteps in sports, but would much rather spend a day at The American Girl Store than at the ESPN Zone.

* * *

The Queen and I met in 1985 when we were undergraduates at Cornell University, and we have now shared more than half a lifetime together. Technically, this is our second voyage as parents. From 1990-1992, we spent the first two years of our marriage as house parents at the Cornell chapter of Delta Delta Delta

Sorority. So in a sense we had about one hundred adopted teenage daughters prior to having "only" four biological ones. One might argue that I should have been prepared. But there is a lot that happens between birth and age nineteen, and at the beginning of this narrative the girls are 8, 8, 8 and 5. So we'll just have to see how it turns out together...

Year 1 - Ages 8, 8, 8 and 5

1. Getting Ready

January, Year 1

Preparing to go somewhere as a family used to be relatively uncomplicated. My wife would hand me various articles of clothing, and I would slip them onto the appropriate appendages of our toddlers and preschoolers. The only challenges were (a) the sheer quantity of said appendages, and (b) remembering which outfit went with which child - often made easier with triplets by purchasing three of the same outfit. At some point the children insisted on dressing themselves. I assumed that would make things even easier on me. Oh really?

* * *

The Scene: Family is preparing to go to worship services. Four daughters are scrambling to get ready on time. Mother calls out "5 minutes!!!" from downstairs.

Daughter #3 *(panicked)*: "Daddy, my tights don't feel right. Can you help me find the right size?"

Father: "I don't know anything about tights. They all look the same crumpled up in your drawer."

D3: "But you know all about sizes and stuff."

Father *(trying to be helpful)*: "What size are you?"

D3: "Daaaadddddyyyy!"

Father: "Look, I really don't know anything about girls' stockings. I don't wear them," *(then adding, in a flash of brilliance)* "just like you don't know anything about underwear with a fly in the front."

Daughter #2 *(arriving on the scene)*: "A what?"

Father *(too much time spent in locker rooms – clearly oblivious to warning signs)*: "A fly in the front."

D2 & D3 *(unison)*: "We don't get it."

Father: "You know how your underwear is flat across, but your jeans have a zipper? Well, boys..." *(suddenly senses magnitude of tactical blunder)* "Oh, never mind." *(Hastily retreats to master bedroom and closes door.)*

D3 *(through the door)*: "Oh, now I get it!"

Father *(also through the door)*: "I'm sure I don't want to know! Go downstairs and tell your mother you need help."

* * *

Of course, lest you think that the only obstacle to getting out the door in the Garden of Estrogen is getting my <u>daughters</u> ready, the following proves that adults can be just as interesting.

The Scene: Getting ready to go out for the evening. The babysitter and the kids are downstairs.

Wife: "Are you going to wear *that?*"

I never know how to answer a question like this. Do I say "Yes" and admit that I am a total fashion ignoramus, or say "No" and admit that I have purposely dressed in clothes I have no intention of wearing? Instead I take the middle ground, hoping to use shame as a weapon.

Husband: "Well, you bought me these clothes for my birthday."

Wife *(ignoring the comment)*: "Put on something else."

Back to the closet, get a different shirt, put it on. Present myself again.

Wife *(casts a withering look)*: "You've got to be kidding."

Husband: "What? You bought me this, too."

The solution is now obvious. I strip to my underwear and sit down on the bed.

Husband: "Let's cut to the chase – just give me anything to put on so that you are willing to be seen with me."

For 360 days out of the year I have no problem dressing myself. For the other five I am apparently missing the critical fashion gene. Having now been properly attired one would think that we are all set to go. However, we are just getting warmed up.

Wife: "This outfit looks terrible."

Husband: "Wait a minute – didn't you just pick out these clothes for me 30 seconds ago?"

Wife: "Not you, me! This outfit looks terrible."

Husband *(trying the same tactics from the last time)*: "You look great. I bought you that outfit last year for your birthday."

Wife: *(ignores brilliant observation - flurry of clothes, new outfit)*: "I still look ridiculous."

Husband *(holding up yet another outfit)*: "How about this one?"

Wife *(another withering look)*: "You've got to be kidding."

In any event, three changes later, we're finally ready to go. What have I learned from this episode? Clearly, neither of us has any clue how to get dressed.

* * *

Then again, perhaps it is hereditary…

<u>Setting:</u> *Monday morning, older daughters getting ready for school. Outfits are laid out on the beds.*

Chorus of three female voices: "Mom, we can't wear that – it looks ridiculous!!!"

2. Jacob and Rachel

February - Valentine's Day, Year 1

Not all Postcards deal with specific personal incidents. Sometimes it is more fun to make observations using fictitious settings. Valentine's Day frequently offers such an opportunity.

* * *

A recipient of my "Postcard" series, who is also a Presbyterian pastor, once observed that the biblical story of Jacob (see "Instant Bible Refresher" at the end of this chapter) might be slightly analogous to mine, given the number of women in Jacob's life. While I'm sure there were certain advantages to having all those wives and mistresses (witness the number of children Jacob produced), the logistics alone had to have been rather daunting. Imagine the following conversation that I am almost certain took place around 3000 B.C.:

The Scene: The patio at Jacob's house, February 14. Jacob is sipping a beer and listening to a hockey game between the Jerusalem Artichokes and the Bagdad Ziggurats.

Leah (wife #1): "Jake, Jake, Jake..." *(turns down the radio)* "You never bring me flowers anymore."

Jacob: "Yes I do - just last week as a matter of fact."

Leah: "No, that was your 5th wife, the cook. And besides, *flour* doesn't count. It's not even the same word in Hebrew!"

Jacob: "What about the Lilly?"

Leah: "She's the handmaiden, not a flower. And to whom did you give her?"

Rachel (wife #2): "What is all the commotion about?"

Jacob: "Nothing dear..."

Leah: "Does he ever bring you flowers? You're his favorite - if anyone would get them it's you."

Rachel: "Nothing. Last year on Valentine's Day all he gave me was a Blockbuster Stone Tablet gift certificate for three free papyrus scrolls. But he forgot to return them and we owed 50 Shekels in late fees!"

Jacob: "Oy vay! What I put up with. I should think I would be appreciated, considering Valentine's Day hasn't even been invented yet."

Rachel: "Don't give us any of that Yiddish - that hasn't been invented yet either. What I really wanted was flowers."

Leah: "Me too."

Rachel: "You are such a Neanderthal."

Jacob: "I'm sure in 5,000 years that will be an insult, but right now we have cousins in France who are Neanderthals - on your mother's side I believe."

Both: "You can sleep in the dog house tonight."

Jacob: "The dog house? Oh well. Someone tell my 7th wife Miriam (the veterinarian) that I'm free tonight after all."

Instant Bible Refresher: *Having enraged his brother Esau by stealing his inheritance, Jacob fled to what is now modern day Iraq to get away. There he met and fell in love with Rachel. Rachel's father Laban convinced him to work for seven years to earn Rachel's hand. Jacob completed the seven years, only to be tricked by Laban into marrying Rachel's older and presumably less desirable sister Leah (note to bachelors – take a good look through the veil before saying "I do"). Jacob got Rachel in the end but had to work another seven years. However, despite having to wait for his true love, Jacob does not seem to have been pining away. Between his various wives and their maids (who doubled as his mistresses), he had 13 children in all – 12 sons and one daughter. Only Joseph – he of the Technicolor Dreamcoat - and Benjamin were born to Rachel, and they came fairly late in the game.*

3. Inventory Day

March, Year 1

Recently the girls and I had Inventory Day. OK, it wasn't really supposed to be Inventory Day. It was supposed to be a day for my wife to do some shopping - alone. Either way, I was left watching four girls, it was raining, and I needed an hour to get some work done.

I had noticed that their vanity (translation for guys – this looks like a desk, but has all manner of grooming paraphernalia) was literally overflowing with "hair stuff" that needed to be cleaned up. In order to make the job more fun, I declared it Inventory Day. The girls would sort and count all the various bows and bands, put them neatly into the drawers, and provide me with a tally at the end of the process.

The official results (yes, it took the full hour):

198 – Thin Bands of Various Sizes and Colors: these are basically miniature bungee cords formed into a circle with a metal sleeve closing the loop.

37 – Scrunchies: large soft/puffy elastic bands with different colors/designs for holding ponytails in place.

66 – Ribbons: the purpose of ribbons is to untie themselves, eliciting a "Do you know how long it took to make that bow?" from the mother.

53 – Clips: these look like part butterfly, part medieval torture device, and are apparently used when a scrunchie is too symmetrical.

13 – Bandanas: I thought only John Wayne and the daughters in Fiddler on the Roof wore these, but it turns out the girls really look cute in them.

22 – Hard Plastic Head Bands: Remember the Brady Bunch? Exactly.

12 – Soft Head Bands: These large elastics are the exclusive adornment of Daughter #2. They are also a popular weapon when shot like a giant rubber band.

Grand Total: 401

These results were rather astonishing (at least to me). I couldn't believe that in a few short years, four little girls could accumulate so much stuff for their hair, especially while I'm so busy losing mine.

It turns out, however, that this is pretty typical. According to my neighbor, who has two daughters, all girls have hundreds of these things. So let's do the math:

4 girls, ages 8, 8, 8, 5, and 400 individual pieces (100 per). Since they didn't have all that much hair until they were beyond their first birthday, this means that each child has been accumulating pieces at a rate of about 15 per year. If the trend continues, by age 38 (my guess at

the median age of an American female), they will have nearly 600 pieces each. Given that The Queen is about at the median age, this could explain the disappearance of the top surfaces of several pieces of bedroom furniture. There are 150 million women in the USA. Even accounting for the occasional Annie Lennox crew cut (and ignoring bobby pins), that's something like *90 billion* female hair implements nationwide!

* * *

The day after Inventory Day, with the magnitude of the aforementioned accumulation still swirling in my head, Daughter #3 asked if it's cool that some girls get earrings in their nose or belly button. I nearly passed out.

4. Shower Time

April, Year 1

Yesterday I stepped into the shower and inadvertently caused an avalanche of plastic bottles. As I set them back up on the edge of the tub, I discovered that there are 19 different bottles of various body and hair care products in my bathroom. To me this is pretty amazing, considering that none of them are mine, except for the bottle of *Pert Plus* shampoo I share with my wife.

I realize that hair is not exactly my strong suit. I have slightly more of it than Bruce Willis, while the five women I live with can each audition for the part of "Cousin It" in the next remake of The Addams Family.

But I digress - the point of this Postcard is not the state of my hairline, but rather the process by which the aforementioned 19 bottles get used. Due to the presence of so much hair in our house, shower night is consistently a "limits testing event." What limits, you ask?

- One 40 gallon water tank and soaring fuel costs – which act as strong disincentives when considering a new 80 gallon tank.
- 3 gallons per minute shower head (at 2/3 hot and 1/3 cold, this means about 20 minutes of hot water)
- One 8 year old who has a prematurely developed sense of privacy
- One 5 year old who has no sense of time and only a marginal ability to rinse the shampoo from her hair on the first try
- Two parents' patience

You do the math. If everyone cooperates and at least two double up, we can sometimes make it. However, adding to the chaos is the presence of a few canisters of "shower foam" – colored foam, the purpose of which seems to be to simultaneously decorate the walls and diminish the inventory of hot water. The 5 year old absolutely loves this stuff. As chief shower enforcer, I have some rather stern words for Santa the next time I see him.

The end result is usually that the last one in gets a one night membership in the Polar Bear Club (and has to clean out the drain).

Needless to say, if we are all going out for the evening and a shower is required, I make sure I am either strategically first, or that enough confusion exists among the five ladies in the house that we are sufficiently delayed for the hot water to return. Fortunately, when I don't shower first I have noticed that the confusion seems to take care of itself (see Postcards #1 and #2). As a result, I rarely have to instigate.

I can't even fathom what will happen when they start shaving their legs.

In a later chapter: an actual scene from Shower Night in the Garden of Estrogen. Note: some portions may not be suitable for the fainthearted.

5. Modesty

May, Year 1

Over the course of the last year, Daughter #1 has become the first to acquire extreme modesty when it comes to changing clothes or taking showers. This is not so much directed at me – I'm happy to stay out of her way at these times - but at her sisters. It got me musing…

* * *

Did it really take a serpent and an apple to convince us that wearing clothes most of the time is a good idea? I think we would have figured that one out on our own – or didn't they have bugs, thorns, and poison ivy in Eden? What Adam and Eve did by partaking of the forbidden fruit was to guarantee that taking OFF our clothes would be forever enticing.

It's an interesting process we go through. We are born completely nude and we don't care. At some point, like Daughter #1, we go from this original state to our "natural" state of modesty. We need this to happen in order to avoid ending up dancing on tables in a sleazy bar. However, once we get modesty, we begin a full cycle that goes a little like this:

- We are very reluctant to remove clothing around members of the opposite sex (or in the case of most females, members of the same sex as well).
- Then we meet the love of our life. Suddenly we shed clothes as quickly and often as possible.
- All this shedding of clothing comes with a side effect – babies.
- Eventually babies become children, gaining an awareness of their surroundings.
- This causes parents to cover up again.
- This re-acquisition of clothing ultimately leads to a cessation of the baby production process long before it is biologically dictated.

In my case, as the lone male in the tribe (pound chest – emit Tarzan yell), I am the only one who must cover up at all times. However, the effect on baby production seems to be just as pronounced as if both of us were required to do so. Of course there are other influencing factors in this reproductive cessation, such as sudden interrupting knocks on the bedroom door in the middle of the night and, of course, sheer exhaustion. But I think that clothing is definitely at or near the top of the list.

…now you begin to understand why The Queen shudders whenever I start musing.

6. Fashion

June, Year 1

I have heard it said that fathers love to dress up their little girls. I love golf too, but it doesn't mean I'm all that good at it. When it comes to correcting aberrant fashion behavior, the results are even worse. Fortunately for most dads with daughters, there appears to be a natural order of things. Oldest daughter imitates mother, younger daughter imitates older daughter, etc – at least until they become teenagers. With 8 year old triplets, however, something gets messed up, and I seem powerless to correct it.

The Scene: Getting ready for school.

D2 appears wearing two headbands simultaneously.

Father: "Why are you wearing two headbands?" *(I really need to learn to stay out of these situations. Has anyone seen my golf clubs?)*

D2: "Because I want to."

Father (*applying recent lessons learned from Inventory Day*): "I get it – you have so many you need to double up."

D2: "Huh? (*eyes narrow*) Is this going to be another one of your <u>rules</u>?"

Father (*I think perhaps I have been "dissed" here*): "No, it's just silly. Do you see either one of your sisters wearing two headbands?"

D1 (*appears wearing two different color socks*): "What's wrong with two headbands?"

Father: "I give up. Where is D3?"

As if on cue, D3 bursts into the room wearing a shirt that is so small she looks like she stole it from a Barbie doll.

Father: "You can't wear that shirt. It's too small."

D3 (*pleading*): "But Daddy, it's my favorite."

Father: "Maybe two years ago, but not today. And my name is not 'But Daddy,' it's Daddy." (*I say that a lot – it always causes a classic 'roll the eyes' reaction.*)

By now the problem should be obvious. In my dream world (the one where my golf score is in the 70's), D1 would know how to dress already – i.e., matched socks. D2 might indeed show up with two headbands, but it would prompt D1 to say "Ditch the extra headband. You look like a complete loser!" This would be punctuated by forming a letter L on the forehead with her fingers. The two of them would gang up on D3, etc. I should note for the record (and for my youngest, who will read this someday), D4 actually has a great sense of fashion, always perfectly matched and coiffed even at age 5. However, the older ones routinely ignore her – what does she know? Fortunately, my wife appears just in time to take control of the situation.

Mother: "D2, take off the extra headband or you're not leaving. D3, same for you with the shirt – get one that fits." *(turns to me)* "Honey, how could you let them come downstairs looking like that?"

I stare in speechless amazement – how is this my fault? She obviously has me confused with someone who understands female offspring.

Father *(trying to save face)*: "D1, go get two socks that match."

D1 bursts into tears.

Mother: "Don't be ridiculous. She's just expressing herself." *(tears disappear)*

I am hopelessly lost here. Where are my golf clubs?

7. Driving Preview

July, Year 1

Several nights ago I had the hiccups. All of the usual remedies failed – holding my breath, drinking water, etc. Of course the kids tried to get into the act as well, yelling "BOO!" in my face and wondering why I wasn't startled, not to mention uncured. Finally, Daughter #2 smiled sweetly and said, "Daddy, guess what? I'm going to have my driver's license in 8 years." As the defibrillator was being put away, I noticed that the hiccups were gone.

I think I also had a "flashforward" - not a premonition mind you, but a flashforward. For those of you who have never had one, it is a little like a flashback and just as vivid, except (a) it hasn't necessarily happened yet, (b) it's far scarier, and (c) LSD is not involved. I'm told it is fairly common among fathers of young daughters.

* * *

Dateline, October 8, Eight Years in the Future - D1, D2 and D3 have all earned their drivers licenses on the same day.

What was I thinking?! Why didn't I do what my father did when my sister turned 17 and plan strategic business trips with the family car for about 6 months straight? *"Sorry, Linda, you just can't take the test next Wednesday. I'm going to be in Schenectady. Is that really the only available date for the next 9 weeks? Maybe we can schedule something next year."* My dad was brilliant.

Having received their licenses, the girls now ask for a car – that would be one for each of them. For a moment, let's put aside the fact that in exactly one year I will be mortgaging my entire existence to several universities. Now assume I have taken momentary leave of my senses and am willing to even entertain this notion. I contemplate for a second, regain my sanity, and respond with a caring, sensitive, "NO!" (Note: uncaring and insensitive would have been "Are you all nuts?")

Not to be deterred, and having perfected the art of negotiation as teenagers, they will make a seemingly magnanimous concession and offer to accept a single car for the three of them. The answer is still a sensitive and caring "NO". "But Daddy," *(they will still call me that)* "we'll <u>share</u> the car." After repeating for the millionth time that my name is not "But Daddy," I will point out that they have never successfully shared anything since the womb, and that doesn't count because:

   a) they had no choice
   b) they could not speak
   c) they had a habit of kicking the daylights out of
     my wife's insides, which does not exactly qualify
     as evidence of serene cohabitation

And now, if they get upset at each other over the sharing of an enclosed space, that space will be moving along the highway at 55 miles per hour.

The discussion is at a stalemate, which is good for me since a tie means no transportation. This condition persists until D3, who undoubtedly has a law degree in her future, brightens and says, "Never mind, Daddy. My boyfriend just got his license, too. We'll all go in his car."

The nice salesman at the auto mall gives me three complimentary calendars – one for each car I just purchased.

8. Rookie QB

Football season is almost upon us. It is nearly impossible to turn on the television without encountering a preseason game. Although I love the sport, exhibition football is about as exciting as observing golfers on a driving range. However, as the NFL is responsible for this postcard and, at least indirectly, the names of my first three children, the league deserves its due. I'll explain...

Have you ever noticed that when a rookie NFL quarterback runs out on the field, taped to his non-throwing wrist is a card on which all the plays are written? I'll grant you this was marginally necessary when plays were signaled in from the sidelines. *Hmm, let's see - if the coach blows his nose and flaps his arms like a quail on speed, it means we run a P3-41C with a fly option.* However, all the quarterbacks now have headphones in their helmets and up to 40 seconds with which to communicate to ten other people who have each attended several years of college. At the very least, the coach could just say to the QB while he is in the huddle, "Repeat after me: #32, you go left. #88, you

---

run downfield. The rest of you, block. Like we did in practice, on three – OK, ready, break!!!"

These people don't know <u>real</u> pressure. What's the worst that can happen – interception? In my case, flash back nearly nine years ago to the preparations for the arrival of our triplets. My beloved, as is her style, had carefully orchestrated everything, which was quite a "feet" considering at the time she couldn't see hers. We had the house all ready, the call list made and checked twice, the bags packed, and the names picked out.

Ah, yes, the names! You see, the babies had already been identified as A, B and C through multiple ultrasounds. We were also fairly confident (but not certain) that they would be delivered in that order. What we had NOT done during any of the ultrasounds was peek at the gender of our children. As a result, we not only needed to come up with twelve names (actually eleven, because one middle name turned out to work for either gender), but we had to decide which ones would be used depending on which babies arrived of which sex in which order. Alas, this was one thing my wife could not control, as she would be a bit hazy during the process. This meant that it was entirely up to me to make sure that the right call would be made at the right time for the right baby in the right sequence. My wife was clearly terrified at the prospect of trusting such an important duty to anyone else.

The big morning arrived. We drove to the hospital and they prepped my wife for the C-section. This was the moment all of that time spent watching large men chase a misshapen piece of leather would pay off. I was the quarterback! Dutifully, I taped my "plays" (i.e., the names and the permutations) to my wrist. I was then placed in a holding room to put on a set of scrubs and wait... and wait... and wait. Finally, a nurse appeared, apologizing profusely because they had started the surgery without me, and would I like to join them. *You think????*

Show time! I walked into the delivery room, quickly counted 17 people and two baby warmers (they needed a second room for the other warmer), paused for a glance at surgery in progress – *Now that's something you don't see every day. Hey honey, check this out. I think I can see your spleen. Oh, never mind, you're busy* – stepped carefully over a few tubes and hoses, and took my place next to my wife and the anesthesiologist.

Suddenly it happened. A baby was screaming. It was a girl! I checked the card and dutifully called out "D1" (I did use her actual first and middle name in the hospital). And then another – "D2", and a third – "D3". I did it! Obviously high fiving the anesthesiologist and doing an end zone dance were out of the question in such cramped quarters, so I just smiled, kissed my beloved, whispered something suitable for the occasion and retired to the Triplet Hall of Fame, my place in history secure.

9. Crying in Baseball, Cartwheels in Soccer

September, Year 1

"There is no crying in baseball!"
- Jimmy Dugan (Tom Hanks), in *A League of Their Own*.

Such a simple statement, really, and yet profound. At one time, baseball was a game played almost exclusively by men, under rules of men's behavior. Idolized by young boys, envied by other men, sought after by women, a star baseball player stood at the pinnacle of the American athletic scene. There was no room in the game for anything but undiluted testosterone. Hence, no crying in baseball.

The period depicted in *A League of their Own* was World War II America. The men were off fighting, and women's teams were organized to keep the sport alive and the fans entertained in their absence. But the introduction of women to this all-male sport came at a price – there was, apparently, crying in baseball.

Is that such a bad thing? Nowadays, a player hits a game winning home run to clinch the World Series, and he can't get three words out between sobs. On the other hand, that same player is also making about $10 million a year, and the home run just gave him $10 million more, so maybe I would cry too – right along with my tearful agent, Jerry Maguire.

I can hear you now. "What prompted this odd musing?"

* * *

I have been involved in soccer (football for my international readers) for most of my life – player, fan, and more recently, coach. My grandfather was a semi-pro player, so it must be in the genes. To be honest, my first passion among team sports is ice hockey. Nevertheless, I like soccer in part because it is unambiguous: no pads (unless you want to count those little shin guards), no stop time, big ball, big goal, very few rules. There is only one type of scoring, the occurrence of which sets off a scene that bears a strong resemblance to a prison break (and in the English Premier League, this may not be far from actual fact).

Soccer tends to be played by some pretty tough people – mostly men at first, but as women have taken up the game, I have noticed they tend to be some pretty tough customers as well (ever see the look in Mia Hamm's eyes?). It therefore came as a bit of a surprise to me as I began coaching my daughters three years ago that girls' soccer at the youngest levels appears to suffer from an abundance of cartwheels.

At first I thought perhaps the cartwheel craze was merely a result of the specific collection of girls on my daughters' team. However, as I have talked to other dads and observed their teams in action, the cartwheel infestation is approaching epidemic stage. At any point in time on a soccer field, whether during practice or a game, a percentage of the faces can be found upside down – and it is frequently the most skilled players who are so oriented. I wonder if we should be putting cleats on their hands and shin guards on their forearms. During one of D4's recent kindersoccer games, the parents sat in stunned amusement as a player cartwheeled *over* the ball in play!

And so, as fathers and coaches we must act promptly, lest we lose some of these multi-talented female athletes to cheerleading or some other sport that is designed to prematurely attract the males of the species (our true concern).

If you are a father, uncle, older brother, or coach of a young female soccer player, we desperately need your help in spreading the word. Ask Tom Hanks for help if you can get him:

> *There are no cartwheels in soccer!!!*
> *There are no cartwheels in soccer!!!*
> *There are no cartwheels in soccer!!!*

Anyone caught violating this rule will take heading practice using a mesh bag full of cold oatmeal.

10. SHOWER TIME - THE SEQUEL

OCTOBER, YEAR 1

In Chapter 4, I promised a glimpse into an actual shower night in the Garden of Estrogen.

* * *

The Scene: Family is downstairs at the dinner table, concluding the meal. The kids were playing outside all afternoon, and it shows from head to toe.

Mother: "OK, shower time everyone."

Daughters (in unison): "Bath."

Mother: "Shower."

Daughters (again, in unison): "Bath!"

Father: "Freezing cold bath."

Daughters: "OK, shower (grumble, grumble)."

Mother: "Now use the potty (the little one sometimes forgets that and suddenly jumps out of the shower halfway through), get your muddy clothes off and into the hamper, and get upstairs."

D1 (the modest one): "Even me?"

Mother: "No, you can get undressed in the bathroom, but only if you get in and out of the shower quickly."

Several minutes pass. Mother is doing laundry. Father walks upstairs. D2 is ready for her shower. D3 is reading, fully dressed. D1 is slowly flossing her teeth, also fully dressed. D4 is playing with her dolls.

Father: "D2, into the shower, now. D3, put the book down, get undressed, and get into the shower." *Note - when D3 starts reading, a tornado could pass through and she would take no notice.*

D1: "Hey, I thought I was supposed to go first."

Father: "You lost your turn. Now you have to wait. D3, put the book down <u>right now</u> and get into the shower." *D3 sheds her clothes and gets into the tub. Father walks back into the hall and shouts,* "D4, where are you! Did you use the potty?"

D4: "I forgot."

Father: "Go now, and then get ready to go in the shower."

D2: "I'm done!" *Steps out of the shower, water cascading everywhere. Father, knowing what to expect, comes back in to wipe up the floor. A squeegee would help right about now. What is a little unexpected, however, is to see D3 kneeling at the other end of the tub with her book propped up outside the tub (the book wetter than her body), turning pages as she continues to read.*

Father: "D3, are you reading in the shower?"

D3: "Sort of." *It's really wonderful that this child is such an avid reader, but there are limits. The book is removed from the scene.*

D4: "I'm ready."

Father: "Did you use the potty?"

D4: "I forgot." *Scampers off to the other bathroom.*

Mother *(appearing in the bathroom doorway)*: "D2, there is still conditioner in your hair. You didn't rinse. And you spilled half the conditioner bottle in the bathtub."

D2: "No there isn't, and it wasn't my fault."

Mother: *(picks up D2 and deposits her back in the shower. Turns to father.)* "How could you let her do that? And why is D3's hair still dry?" *Father has learned when not to respond.*

Father: "D4, where are you?!"

D4: "Here, Daddy."

Father: "Why are you still dressed? And where did you get that hat? Now you have more clothes on, not fewer."

D4: "I forgot. And anyway, I'm a fashion model." *Flips blond hair and disappears around the corner.*

D2: "I'm done again." *This time father is ready with a towel and successfully avoids the flood.*

D4 *(finally reappears in her underwear)*: "I'm ready." *Steps into the shower, forgetting to remove her underwear.* "Oops – I forgot." *(giggle – removes soaking underwear and tosses out of the shower, hitting D2, who emits an ear-splitting scream)*

Father *(once ears have stopped ringing from D2's outburst)*: "D3, make sure D4 actually washes herself – and no books in the shower! D1, make sure they both get out of the shower."

D1: "What am I, the mother?"

Father: "No, you are the one who wants a warm shower." *Phone rings. Father answers. A few minutes pass before returning to the scene.*

Father *(calling through the door)*: "D3, are you done?"

D3: "Yes, I'm out now."

Father: "D4, have you even started yet?"

D4: "I forgot." *Is it just me or does anyone else expect Abbott and Costello to start saying "Third Base" right about now?*

D1 and D3 *(in unison)*: "It's not my fault!"
Father grabs a washcloth and cleans D4, then takes her out of the shower, dries her off, and sends her toward her bedroom to get her pajamas. Fortunately, the bathroom was designed anticipating D1's extreme modest streak and has one of those doors between the sink area and the shower/toilet. D1 steps into the inner room and closes the door.

D1 *(about 2 minutes later)*: "**EEEEAAAGHHH!** It's freezing! Why did you make me go last?"

Father *(through the door)*: "You lost your turn, remember?"

D1: "It wasn't my fault!"

Father: "Sorry, can't be helped. D4, do you have your pajamas on?"

OK readers, everyone in unison now for D4: "I FORGOT."

11. Laundry, Physics and Theology

December, Year 1

Irecently attended a religious service where the subject of the sermon was finding light in the darkness. In the book of Genesis, the creation of light is the very first event recorded, without which nothing that followed could possibly have occurred. My friend the Presbyterian pastor confirms that this is a biblical interpretation that should be acceptable to Jews, Christians and Muslims alike. We have therefore established a reasonable theological foundation for our discussion.

The laws of physics also tell us that darkness is the absence of light, and that white light is the presence of all colors. I'm pretty sure I understand this fairly well, if mostly through osmosis. My father actually had a Ph.D. in this field and taught it as a university professor. On the wall of my office hangs one of his prized possessions: a full-color representation of the Electromagnetic Spectrum, from microwaves all the way to gamma rays and everything in between (including visible light). My firsthand knowledge consists of having barely scraped by in three semesters of college physics. But just to make sure - since this light/darkness concept is so very important - I married a former high school physics teacher.

You, of course, are entitled to be a skeptic, unwilling to accept either academia or scripture. If so, here are two simple experiments you can try to convince yourself:

1. Take a circular piece of paper and color equal pie slices of at least red, green and blue. Add more slices of different colors if you like. Next locate a child's spinning top and affix the paper to it. Now wind it up and let it go. The paper turns white (all colors).
2. OK, much simpler – go into a windowless room and turn out the light. You see black.

So we have theology and science. Where does the laundry part come in? I thought you would never ask...

* * *

When we were first married, my wife was attending classes all day in graduate school, and as I was working from a home office I thought it was perfectly reasonable that I handle a share of the laundry. We had received a beautiful set of jet black bath and hand towels as wedding gifts, and one morning she was horrified to see me putting the towels into the same laundry basket as my underwear and socks. I informed her that I had always washed my towels together with my socks and underwear because they both took high heat to dry.

"Do you know what will happen if you put those brand new black towels in with something white?" she asked.

"Don't worry," I said, "that underwear has been washed many times before. Nothing will happen."

"Not the underwear, you fool – the towels. They will bleed on the rest of the stuff in the wash."

I replied with the confidence of a newlywed man of the house (and the aforementioned physics background), "How can black lose any more color? The color is already gone." My wife threw up her hands in despair, obviously wondering at that point if I was pulling her leg or if our nuptial vows contained a stupidity escape clause.

Finally reassuring her, I revealed, "Honey, I already washed them. Nothing happened." This, unfortunately, did not have the desired effect of ending the debate.

She replied, "All that proves is that the folks at Fortunoff were smart enough to buy pre-washed towels. Otherwise there would be a bunch of silly men running around with unintentionally colored underwear."

Not having owned brand new towels before then (when I got my own place my parents gave me a bunch of theirs), I must admit in hindsight that I was extremely lucky not to have ended up with a drawer full of underwear and socks having an ashen hue.

* * *

Fifteen years later, however, I have made a profound discovery which, if published in the right venue, could earn me the Nobel Prize for Physics and set the theological world on its head. It turns out that the absence of color is NOT black, and I have irrefutable evidence to prove it. You see, those same pitch black towels from Fortunoff, after several hundred washings with only other black items, have lost some "color" and are now DARK GRAY!!!

I say, *"A-men!!!!"*

My wife just rolls her eyes and says, "Men."

* * *

My Postcards frequently generate reader responses of some kind – universally positive so far. Sometimes, however, the responses take on a life of their own, and this one was unbelievable. If this chapter amused you, I invite you to turn to the Appendix to see some of the responses.

12. Bathroom Excursions

December, Year 1

Dateline, October 8: Morristown, NJ – 9 years ago.

9:22 am: "It's a girl!"
9:23 am: "It's a boy – no wait, it's another girl!" (Uh, excuse me doc, that's an umbilical cord you're holding.)
9:24 am: "It's another girl! Congratulations - you have three baby girls!"

Some time after that dramatic moment and the subsequent whirlwind of activity, when the babies were weighed, measured, cleaned up and pronounced healthy, I whispered to my beloved, "I win."

I was referring, of course, to the now infamous potty training bargain. When we discovered we were expecting triplets, my wife and I made two promises. One – we would not peek closely at a certain section of the ultrasound and ruin the surprise. Two – I would be responsible for potty training any boys, she would do likewise for any girls. When D4 was born three years later, I had achieved a clean sweep. Victory was mine! Or so I thought...

* * *

My brother has two boys and a girl, 9, 7 and 4 respectively. When they need to go, about all my brother has to do is tell my nephews to remember to square their shoulders. Meanwhile, my sister in-law takes my niece into the women's room. Thirty seconds later, the guys are done and horsing around waiting for the two ladies. So simple!

I, on the other hand, have become a "bathroom pack mule." Whenever the girls have to go, the entirety of the worldly possessions of five females – coats, hats, sweaters, mittens, handbags, shopping bags, etc., become mine for at least the next 15-20 minutes. I am then a source of amusement to anyone passing by:

"Look – a pile of coats with legs."
"Do you think he's with the Salvation Army?"
"That handbag doesn't go with his shoes."
"Hey, Mommy - do you think that man stole all those coats?"
"Here, have another one – where is my claim check?"

The crowning moment (thus far) occurred last winter on a family ski day. The weather was unseasonably warm – high 40's – a great day to be on the slopes. We were planning on skiing the afternoon and into the evening. At about 5:00 pm, the four girls finished their lessons and rejoined us in front of the base lodge. Immediately my wife suggested a bathroom break. I, of course, was back in about 2 minutes. Since I was kind of warm, I grabbed an outside picnic table on the patio of the lodge, whereupon I immediately became the recipient of 10 gloves, 5 hats, 5 goggles, plus four large balloons that the ski school instructors had given the kids to use for learning balance. I was informed in no uncertain terms not to lose the balloons, and my five lovely ladies disappeared into the lodge.

Now what? Have you ever tried to hold four balloons while wearing ski gloves? Of course, just then the breeze picked up, the light started to fade, and the temperature dropped like a stone. Carrying everything inside was impossible. I was able to pin one balloon behind each leg as I sat on the table, and hold the other two – it worked despite the wind as long as I did not move. <u>Thirty minutes</u> later the girls reappeared, looking very warm and refreshed. I, on the other hand, was now frozen solid. My wife took the big three back on the slopes for a few more runs, and I convinced the little one that a cup of hot chocolate by the fire inside would be REALLY nice right about then.

My wife finds all of this very funny. She has a strange sense of humor.

YEAR 2 - AGES 9, 9, 9 AND 6

13. Hair Salon

January, Year 2

When I was a very young child, I remember occasionally having to sit in the "beauty parlor" watching women have strange things done to their hair. The oddest part was when they would have these things that looked like miniature soda cans affixed to their heads (curlers), after which they would sit under these loud, whining, upside-down mixing bowls for what seemed like an eternity. My brother Eric and I were stuck in our own private little boys' purgatory thumbing through the recipes in back issues of *Good Housekeeping* and *McCall's*. I think Eric paid more attention to what he was reading than I, because he has turned out to be a far better cook.

Since my dad cut my hair until I was about 12, I reached adolescence with no first hand basis for comparison to the typical male haircutting experience (i.e., at a real barbershop). However, as Dad would sometimes tell us he was grabbing a quick cut at the airport, it could not have taken very long. But just as I sought non-parental haircutting options (in the late 70's), what formerly were women's beauty parlors

---

became *unisex hair salons*. For some unknown reason, the half of the human race (i.e., men) that had heretofore avoided follicular torture suddenly decided to volunteer for it.

I was apparently mixed up in one aspect of my education, thinking that "unisex" made a person go blind. As a result, I steered exclusively toward haircutting places that had the spiral red, white and blue spinning thing. (Note: evidently, that spinning device posted strategically by the door of a barbershop repels women and "unisexuals.") Fortunately, the 80's arrived just in the nick of time, restoring common sense to male hairlines and giving at least temporary life to the barber community.

* * *

Presently, about 5-6 times a year I shell out $12.00 at the barber shop. Given the size of my forehead these days, that works out on an annual basis to about one dollar per remaining hair, so I have no basis from which to complain about the cost of maintaining proper style. But twice each year, we have "Girls' Hair Day" at the mall salon, which unfolds as follows:

1. My wife informs me what time I need to meet her at the mall after work.
2. I arrive at the mall (slightly late) to a withering glare and am immediately presented with D4. D4, incidentally, although 6 years old, has never had her blond locks cut, but that's an entirely different debate.
3. While I am keeping D4 happy, which usually involves at least one pretzel and a lemonade, my

wife herds the other three through the various phases of wash, cut, dry and style, all the while catching up on things with the stylist (a former neighbor of ours).

4. As each kid finishes up, my responsibility grows. Of course, each child emerges from 30-40 minutes of confinement as if they had just consumed a Starbucks Triple Latte, so I start to feel a bit like the doorman at Wal-Mart on Thanksgiving Friday.

5. Finally, my wife emerges all smiles, instructs me to pay the cashier, and leads the children straight to the mall ice cream store for their "reward."

With my last receipt I got a $5 coupon for my next perm. Somewhere there is a "unisexual" with a nasty sense of humor.

14. Romeo and Juliet

An archeologist searching in England for the ruins of an ancient druid temple recently discovered a box of manuscripts that had been buried for hundreds of years. After an exhaustive study by the respective literature departments at Oxford and Cambridge Universities, the manuscripts have been authenticated as drafts written by none other than William Shakespeare.

Most remarkable was the revelation that the version of Romeo and Juliet that we have come to know is, in fact, the shortened "made for theatre" version. The genuine *R&J Trilogy* is somewhat different. In the original Book I, *A Midsummer Night's Family Feud*, Romeo realizes that Juliet has faked her death and they both flee to Venice, where they settle down to raise a family. Romeo makes a fortune selling gondola insurance, while Juliet raises their SEVEN lovely daughters (and you thought I was outnumbered!)

Here is an excerpt from Book II, entitled *Looking for Two Gentlemen - Try Verona*. As we can see from the dialog, aside from the difficulty of always speaking in verse, Romeo faced his own unique challenges, especially when it came to certain romantic holidays.

PROLOGUE AND DISCLAIMER (*added by yours truly, The Gardener*)

Three Muses appear on stage.

MUSES (*in unison*)
If thy sensibilities be easily offended,
We suggest the reading at this moment be ended.
But if bawdry humor pleases without pretense,
Then partake with us of mirth at poor Romeo's expense.

Muses exit...

The Setting: Venice, Italy, St. Valentine's Day, 1578

JULIET
Romeo O, Romeo,
A soft bed awaits the warmth of our slumber.
The fatigue of the day o'ertakes me,
And sleep's siren song bids us make haste
To fair and blissful repose.

ROMEO
Doth not trifle with my affection,
Juliet my love.
'Tis is the Day of St. Valentine!
Flowers hath I procured.
A romantic feast hath we consumed,
A Blockbuster painting hath we viewed.

JULIET
Romeo my love,
May I be stricken
'Ere I trifle with thy affection.
But wouldst thou believe
I am so easily lured into thine arms?

ROMEO
When seven children hath we produced,
I wouldst think it true.
And yet, I will woo thee as at first.
Come hither, and hear in thine own ears
The sweet caress of my loving whisper.

JULIET
My ears hath been touched but not by thee.
'tis Daughter #5 who rends the stillness of the night
With her fair cry,
And I must soothe her countenance.

ROMEO
There is no need to leave
The warmth of our lair.
D5 merely coos in her chamber,
Where D4 and D6 offer sweet sibling solace.
Dost not mine own countenance need soothing?
Doth not other desires make their presence known?

JULIET
Quite apparent is thy desire
And thy presence.
'Twould be nearly impossible to miss.
Nonetheless, thine own countenance must wait,
Unless self-soothing is what thou wilt.

ROMEO
If thy words be true,
A stake through my heart hast thou driven.
Wouldst thou consign thy beloved to such a fate?
Wouldst thou risk the loss of these eyes
That behold a beauty such as thee?
O, what an inglorious end to an evening
Begun with roses, fair oysters, and truffles,
Upon which a goodly portion of the Montague estate
Hath been laid bare!

JULIET
O, Romeo, your eyesight would not I risk,
But thy patience do I request,
Lest the sounds of the child
Strike the mood from my soul
If she should remain uncomforted.

Juliet exits left.

ROMEO
On St. Valentine's Day indeed!
O, that the privacy we shared
When but two of us there were,
Nary a care in the world
(save our respective families who wanted to kill each
other, but I digress....)
Now steal our moments we must,
When happily coincides
The slumber of little ones.
'Tis a wonder the last were ever conceived!

Juliet returns wearing something very revealing.

ROMEO
O, Juliet,
How I have longed for thee
In thy painful absence.
But do my eyes deceiveth me?
Self soothed have I not!
From whence cometh thy garment,
Barely visible in the moonlight?

JULIET
My garb cometh
From my dear friend, Victoria.
Come to me now, my love,
And knowest thou her secret!

ROMEO
Ah, Venice!!!

EPILOGUE

Three Muses re-appear on stage.

MUSES (*in unison*)
We can see by thy faces
That some of thee are shocked.
But we warned thee,
And did not simply go off half-cocked.
So before telling Shakespeare
Who might be tempted to sue,
You should see our rendition
Of *The Taming of the Shrew!*

Muses Exit.

---

15. KISSING

MARCH, YEAR 2

I think my wife and I tend to be more restrictive than most parents when it comes to the TV shows and movies we let the kids watch. In addition, from a very young age – perhaps it's a triplet thing, or the lack of male siblings – our girls have tended to spook a little easily when watching movies.

So when we decided that the kids were ready for the Disney movie "Aladdin," we kept a close eye to make sure no one was unhappy, particularly the little one (who is only six). We needn't have worried. They loved the movie in spite of the giant serpent, the evil wizard, and the haunting voices – that is, until the very end. As the story drew to a close, the two main characters embraced in a deep, romantic (albeit animated) kiss, which completely freaked out the kids:

- "Eeww, gross!"
- "They are sucking on each others' lips!"
- "I'm never going to do that!"
- "Do you think they let their tongues touch?"

- "That's disgusting when boys and girls share each others' spit."

Naturally my wife and I felt compelled to kiss just then in order to elicit a reprise from the peanut gallery. As the gagging noises subsided, I turned to the girls and said, "I'm delighted you feel that way right now. But you realize that if your mother and I didn't kiss, none of you would be here. If you don't kiss, you can't have kids."

"Why not?" asked D1.

I responded, "Well…"   *I really need to avoid these situations. Anyone seen my golf clubs?*

After letting me twist long enough to be grateful for the intervention, my beloved chimed in, "Because if you don't kiss, God won't know that you love each other."

Sounds good enough for me. Let's come back to this conversation - in about 15 years.

16. SPORTS ILLUSTRATED SWIMSUIT EDITION

APRIL, YEAR 2

Shortly before I turned 13 (in late 1976), I received a holiday gift from my Aunt Laura and Uncle Ken: a magazine subscription to *Sports Illustrated* (a.k.a. "SI"). As there was no Internet – with or without Al Gore – and no ESPN, this weekly periodical provided my best look into the sporting world. The pictures were excellent, as one might expect from a Time-Life publication, and the articles were many and varied. My brother and I diligently read every issue from cover to cover. Thirty years later I am still a subscriber, and now my girls love *SI for Kids*.

One day in February 1977, shortly after the Super Bowl, I received a most welcome surprise. Gracing the cover of my copy of SI was a picture of Christie Brinkley in a beautiful one-piece bathing suit. What did this have to do with sports? I didn't care – I was 13, and she was the most beautiful woman I had ever seen to that point (I didn't meet The Queen until eight years later). In fact, inside the magazine there were dozens of pictures just like that one, showing off different types of swimwear on Miss Brinkley and several other supermodels. For some reason, my ten year old brother didn't seem quite as interested. He wanted to know where were the articles on baseball's upcoming spring training. He would eventually learn the error of his ways.

As I got older I learned that the SI Swimsuit Issue was an annual ritual. The sadness at the departed football season and the cold snowy winter were considerably mitigated by the sight of scantily clad women frolicking in tropical sunshine. Of course in the weeks following this issue, the Letters to the Editor were filled with rants against *Sports Illustrated* for subjecting its readers to such immorality. Invariably there would be a letter from a pastor at some church out in Idaho or Utah saying "I have been a subscriber for 15 years, and I am appalled! Please cancel my subscription." I can only assume that the pastor's sons had been stealing the swimsuit issue for the previous 14 years, and this shocking discovery coincided with the youngest son's freshman year at a distant college.

Over the years, the pictures have become more numerous and more risqué. SI has even taken to body painting, which essentially means covering a few square centimeters of skin with colored paint in order to appear to be a bathing suit.

However, as I have gotten older – perhaps as a result of marrying a six foot tall Greek Goddess, or perhaps because Christie Brinkley, Elle Macpherson, and Kathy Ireland are no longer regularly featured – I have found myself skimming the magazine rather than studying it. In fact, I must confess that I didn't even remember seeing this year's edition... until last weekend.

I was trying to catch up on some work on Saturday morning, when suddenly I heard shrieking from upstairs. Thinking perhaps there was a rhinoceros loose in the house, I called to the girls, "What's wrong up there?" They poured down the staircase, practically tumbling in a mass of arms and legs, screaming "Eeww, gross!!!" OK, now I'm figuring they saw a large bug. Instead, D3 was holding a copy of the latest SI Swimsuit Issue. On the cover were eight supermodels, clad only in white bikini bottoms, with their arms shielding enough of their tops to keep it reasonably mild.

D2: "They're naked!!!"

D4: "Disgusting!"

Father: "I was wondering if they had sent one this year. Wow, is that *Elle Macpherson* on the cover?"

All Girls (*in unison*): "Who's Elle Macpherson?"

Father (*coolly*): "Never mind. What's the problem?"

Frankly, this isn't really a conversation I wanted to be having with my daughters, especially since my wife was out running an errand. I figured if I played it nonchalant the whole thing would blow over. However, in retrospect, perhaps showing a sudden interest in a semi-topless Elle Macpherson wasn't such a good idea. I attempted to change the subject.

Father: "Speaking of swimming, did you know that fish have to wait twenty minutes after eating before they can go back in the water?"

D1: "That doesn't make any sense!"

D3 *(thumbing through the magazine, not so easily deterred)*: "Look at these pictures. All these women are naked. And look at this one. She's just wearing bottle caps!"

Father: "That's not one of the pictures, that's an advertisement."

D3: "What's the difference?"

D1: "They want you to buy something."

D3: "Well, I'm not buying *that*."

Father: "Maybe not, but I can think of a couple of million people who are."

D3: "Like who?"

Father: "Like <u>whom</u>? Use proper grammar." *(See the attempt to change the subject again? It didn't work this time either.)*

D2 *(looking at one of the very busty supermodels striking a pose on a sailboat)*: "I'm really bummed. Soon I'm going to look like her – I don't want to."

Now what was I supposed to say to that? Of course she will be happy to look that good, although if she does end up resembling Daniela Pestova in a swim-suit, I think I would prefer she appear in SI for setting a world record in the 400m Freestyle.

D4: "I don't want to look like her either. I want to look like Mommy!" *(Mommy walks through the door)* "Oh – hi, Mommy."

Mother *(having no idea what is going on, but sensing that she has been "dissed")*: "What's going on here?"

Father: "D4, I really don't think you meant what you just said, but I give up. " *(I hand my wife the magazine.)* "Honey, you explain all of this to the girls. I'm going running... Hey kids, next week maybe David Wright will be on the cover – in his New York Mets uniform. Bye!"

Girls: "COOL!!!"

17. The Hotel Fox

May, Year 2

Copenhagen, Denmark

To my beloved Queen of the Garden of Estrogen,

Greetings from across the ocean, and fear not. I will return in plenty of time for Mother's Day!

You would not believe the unusual hotel I am staying in here in Copenhagen. The Hotel Fox is apparently called an "art hotel", and I have come to understand it is quite famous among the eclectic set. Each room has been separately designed by an artist to have a special theme. I am not sure how they arrived at these themes, but let's just say these artists are far more likely to be showing their paintings at the Museum of Modern Art than at the Met. Of course I knew nothing of this beforehand. As far as I was concerned, this could be Copenhagen's version of a Holiday Inn.

When I checked in, the girl at the reception desk handed me the key with a twinkle in her piercing blue eyes (I guess first timers are easy to spot). Upon

---

arriving at the designated door, the card under the room number announced that the official name of the room was "Sleep Seasons." I opened the door and peered into a narrow entrance hallway that looked like Kermit the Frog meets *The Hitchhiker's Guide to the Galaxy* - all blue and green swirls. The closets all opened from this hall. When I turned the corner into the main room, my jaw REALLY dropped. The main room was done in a combination of browns, oranges, and pinks. A very modern flat screen Samsung TV was mounted on the wall at a height of six inches from the floor! There were no chairs on the brown carpet, just orange ottomans. There was no desk, only a stainless steel tray with feet. And in the middle of the room where the bed was supposed to be, there was a big brown tent, complete with lanterns! Pulling back the flaps revealed a carnation comforter over a futon mattress. I just stood there in disbelief for a few minutes. At least the bathroom looked normal.

I suppose after a few pints of Carlsberg I could manage to deal with the tent, but the lack of a desk combined with my inability to sit cross-legged would make it pretty much impossible to do any work. And besides, that many Carlsbergs might make it hazardous to lie down.

After staring at the room for a time, I returned to the reception desk and asked Miss Twinkle if she realized there was a tent in my room where the bed was supposed to be. She nodded yes. I then asked if my colleagues had specifically requested this room for me or whether it was the only one available. She said it was the latter, but as she suddenly found another, I suspect Miss Twinkle is covering for the wagering that may or may not be taking place among my colleagues over whether I would accept the room.

So now I am sitting in a new room. This one is called "Look At." It is almost completely white. There is definitely a bed (white linens and comforter), white nightstands, and even white cube lights on the nightstands. There is also a stylish white desk of sorts (no drawers - looks like it came from IKEA), but the "chair" is a white cube with no back. The only adornments that break up the white of the room are: i) the flat screen TV on the desk; ii) something written in Danish around a kind of zebra pattern that forms a big circle on the carpet; and iii) a giant black and white mural taking up the whole wall facing the foot of the bed. The mural is entirely of a woman from the shoulders up. Her long hair is flying out and up as if she just hopped off a fence or is lying down on a bed. I suspect she is lying down, because her expression looks like Meg Ryan's in the delicatessen scene from *When Harry Met Sally*. If you think I am jumping to conclusions here, the room description also recommends that I check out the rooms entitled "Sensuality" and "Ecstasy." Perhaps I'll wait for the next time we visit Copenhagen together to try one of those rooms!

So there you have it - at least two of the rooms at the famous Hotel Fox. To see the rest, go to http://www.hotelfox.dk and click on ROOMS. You will find my old room (#121) and my new room (#111 – complete with "Deli Lady") on the link called MEDIUM. There you can click on each room and assure yourself that I have not been sampling too many of the local beers.

Perhaps we should invent a "children's art" hotel.

Each guest family checks into a white room with a supersized box of Crayolas.

Anyway, if you need me, call the front desk and ask Miss Twinkle for the guy who didn't like the tent.

Faithfully yours,

The Gardener

18. Old Navy

June/July, Year 2

OK men – did you ever wonder what happens inside the female dressing room at a clothing store? For this installment, I have called upon the services of my lovely wife, The Queen of the Garden of Estrogen, to accurately describe what we men cannot know.

*   *   *

I have a recurring nightmare...

It's Sunday, a beautiful summer day. I have been traveling a lot lately, and I am looking forward to relaxing at home and watching a New York Mets baseball game with the girls. My wife has other plans. It seems the three big girls need some new clothing for the upcoming school year and she wants to go to Old Navy. I absolutely hate clothes shopping, even for myself (fortunately, my body shape apparently approximates that of a mannequin, because I can usually pull shirt, pants, and even a jacket right off the rack and be done in about 10 minutes). However, on this occasion I step out of character and agree to go – the Golfsmith store is right next to Old Navy, and I want to look at some clubs. Big mistake! Upon parking the car, my wife insists that I come into the clothing store and hang outside the dressing room so that she can go inside, sending the girls out for refills from the racks.

With nothing else to do, I catch up on e-mails on my Black-berry. One of these days I have to figure out some of the other things this gadget can do.

THE SCENE INSIDE THE DRESSING ROOM

Mother: "D1, try these pants on."

D1 *(the modest one)*: "Not in front of my sisters."

Mother: "Fine, use the next stall."

D3 *(buttoning a pair of blue jeans)*: "I'm not sure if these fit."

Mother: "Are they too tight?"

D3: "Kind of."

Mother: "Go get the next bigger size. Take D2 with you." *D2 and D3 exit. D4 has been rummaging through the pile of clothes waiting to go back on the racks.*

D4: "Mommy, look! I found a cool outfit."

Mother: "You don't need any new clothes today. Put those back please."

MEANWHILE, OUTSIDE THE DRESSING ROOM

Father: "Hi kids. Any luck?"

D3: "I need to get the next size."

D2: "Are the Mets winning?"

Father: "How would I know? I'm stuck here in a clothing store."

D2 and D3 take more clothes into the dressing room. I return to the Blackberry and start to explore some of the other functions – "one of these days" is today. Hey, there's a browser on this thing! I wonder if it has sports scores. It does - COOL!!!

INSIDE THE DRESSING ROOM

D1: "Moooooom! (that's a short 'o' – does not rhyme with 'moose'), I can't get these on."

Mother: "I'm coming. Which stall are you in? Oh, there you are. Well no wonder – you have them on backwards. Take them off."

D4 *(appearing at the stall door)*: "Mommy look – a glitter shirt."

D1: "Get her out of here. She's looking at my underwear!"

Mother: "D4, go put that back. I said no new clothes today. D1, stop yelling and close the door."

D2: "Mom, look at this great sweat jacket I found."

Mother: "That's cute, but you were supposed to be looking for pants. And where's D3?"

OUTSIDE THE DRESSING ROOM

D4 is now rummaging through a rack. While intently reviewing the baseball scores, I overhear two Old Navy sales associates talking about the lady in the dressing room taking up four of the six stalls.

D3 *(holding up a pair of white pants and a matching white shirt)*: "Daddy, do you think Mommy will like these?"

Father *(not looking up)*: "I'm sure she'll love it. Tell D2 that the Mets are in a rain delay in the 4th tied 3-3, but David Wright is 2 for 2 with a home run."

D2 emerges from the dressing room, hears the update, gives D3 a high five, grabs a pair of pants, and they head back in together with D4.

INSIDE THE DRESSING ROOM

D1 *(four pairs of pants later)*: "These don't feel good either."

Mother: "What's wrong now, too tight?"

D1: "No."

Mother: "Too loose?"

D1: "No."

Mother: "Well, what's the problem?"

D1: "I don't know, I think maybe one of the sequins itch."

Mother: "The sequins are on the outside of the *pocket* - how could they possibly itch?"

D1: "I don't know. Do you think I should get them?"

Mother: "Not if they itch. Take them off." *D1 removes the pants and hands them out.* "Too bad - these come in three different colors."

D1: "I don't know. Maybe they don't itch..."

Mother *(looking skyward)*: "The Princess and the Pea has nothing on this one."

D4: "Mommy, look - a purple blazer and mini-skirt, just my size!"

Mother: "D4, we are NOT buying you any more clothes. With all the great stuff you got from your sisters, your cousins, plus your own stuff, you don't have enough room in your drawers as it is." *(D4 pretends to pout and slinks away – she seems to be the only one truly enjoying herself.)*

D3 *(now resplendent in a pair of white pants and a sweater)*: "Hi, Mom. Look at these. They fit perfectly."

Mother: "You've got to be kidding. Do you have any idea how impossible it will be to keep those white pants and sweater clean?"

D3: "I'll be careful."

Mother: "Not negotiable. Go find something else."

D2: "All set, Mom. I found 5 pairs of blue jeans that fit."

Mother: "That's great, but you can't wear only blue jeans. How about some regular pants?"

D2: "Yuk!"

D4: "Mommy look…"

Mother: "I don't want to see it. Put it back. D1, have you made a decision?"

D1: "I don't know."

Mother: "That's the eighth pair you have tried on. Something has to appeal to you."

D1: "I don't know."

OUTSIDE THE DRESSING ROOM

D3: "Daddy, what's negotiable?"

Father: "Apparently everything except whether I can leave this store to look at golf clubs."

D3: "Huh?"

D2: "Daddy, Mommy won't let me wear blue jeans."

D3: "You mean she won't let you wear ONLY blue jeans."

D2: "Who asked you? Daddy, what's the score of the Mets game now?"

Father: "Last I checked, the Mets were up 5-3 in the 7th. They just took out Pedro Martinez."

INSIDE THE DRESSING ROOM

D3 *(holding up a pair of pants)*: "Mommy, these fit. I'm going to look for a matching sweater."

Mother: "Wait – I want to see them. Go put them on again."

D2 *(miraculously wearing something NOT made of denim)*: "How are these?"

Mother: "Looks good. If they fit, put them on the door and try on the next pair. D3, how could you say those pants are OK? They are two inches too short."

D3: "That's the style."

Mother: "Too small. Try the other pair on."

D3 *(holding up a different pair)*: "But I want these."

Mother: "Those are green. What do you own that goes with those?"

D3: "Lots of things."

Mother: "Name one. Otherwise try these." *(hands her several other pairs)*

D2: "These fit too. And look, I found a bouncy ball in the stall." *(D2 proceeds to ricochet the ball off two doors, a mirror, and a wall.)*

Mother: "Good, you are done. Now put down that ball immediately before you break something. D1, have you made a decision?"

D1: "I don't know."

D4: "Look Mommy, a fuzzy robe and a pair of Strawberry Shortcake socks!"

Mother: "You already have three robes from your sisters. But since you have been in such a good mood this entire time, if you would like the socks, it's OK with me." *(D4 is delighted.)*

D3: "The black ones fit, and so do the blue ones. The sweater fits, too."

Mother: "Hallelujah! OK, you're done. D1, decision time NOW."

D1: "I still don't know."

Mother: "Five seconds, 4, 3, 2, 1..."

D1: "OK, I'll take them."

OUTSIDE THE DRESSING ROOM

My wife emerges at last, preceded by all four girls carrying various articles of clothing for purchase. D2 doesn't care about the clothes, but very much wants to know if the Mets won (they did). D4 shows me her new socks and launches into a recap of all the great clothes she tried on. D1 seems not to be particularly thrilled with her selections. D3 is pleased as punch. The sales associates look relieved. We pay for everything, drag the bags out to our minivan, and drive away. My wife looks like she could use a hot shower and an icy margarita. We are halfway home before I realize I never got to the golf store.

* * *

Thankfully, my side of this never actually happened. Knowing how I feel about shopping, my wife would not subject me to such an afternoon. However, the scene <u>inside</u> the dressing room is apparently a condensed version of a two hour episode that actually took place in Old Navy. I think I'll go prepare a very large margarita for my beloved Queen to celebrate both her infinite patience AND her willingness to shed her editor's cap to team up on this Postcard.

19. Makeup - Part A

August, Year 2

I imagine in a few years my house will be the venue for the following scene:

D3 *(to D2 and D1)*: "OK, let's go – everyone's waiting for us at the mall and we don't want to be late."

Father *(looking up from laptop)*: "That never seems to work when the family needs to be somewhere on time. Why start now?" *(suddenly notices something strange)* "Hey, what's that stuff all over your eyes?"

D3: "Nothing, Dad." *(D1 and D2 surreptitiously slip behind D3 – I wonder what they are hiding.)*

Father: "Is that eye shadow and mascara?"

D3: "Maybe a little."

Father: "A little? Why are you wearing anything on your eyes? You aren't even 13 yet! And anyway, the amount you are wearing hardly qualifies as 'a little.'"

D4 (*putting down the book she is reading*): "They are 15, Dad."

Father: "Who asked you? And anyway, who said that 15 is old enough to wear eye makeup to the mall? (*calling upstairs*) Honey, how old were you when you were allowed to wear eye makeup?"

This is really kind of an unfair question, because my wife was born with natural skin coloring and eyelashes that render makeup unnecessary unless we are really getting dressed up. Nevertheless, I need to use any advantage I can get right about now.

Mother: "I never really wore makeup until I got to college."

Father: "You heard it. Now go back and take it off. D1 and D2, let me see your faces."

D1 and D2 step to the side.

Father: "D1, you're wearing makeup, too. Do you know they test that stuff on animals?"

D1 (*our resident animal lover*): "That's stupid. Who wants to see whether a goat looks good in eye shadow?"

Father: "They don't care if the goat looks good, they want to see if the goat dies."

D1: "Eew, that's so mean!" (*running upstairs*) "Where's the makeup remover?"

D2: "They test the makeup remover on animals, too, don't they Dad?"

Father: "Yes, but let's keep that between us. I'm glad to see you are not wearing any makeup, but please get out of your soccer uniform and into some real clothes. You are not going out in shorts and shin guards."

D3 *(trying to salvage something from the exchange)*: "Can I at least wear lip gloss?"

Father: "OK, you can wear the lip gloss. Now get upstairs before I change my mind."

D2 and D3 tromp upstairs. I assume D3 will foolishly reapply the eye makeup when they get to the mall. This will result in her missing the next excursion when the subterfuge is detected. D2 will pull her New York Giants Eli Manning jersey over her top, but that's OK. If she acts like a typical teenage girl at the mall, everyone will blame it all on some father named Manning.

D1 returns downstairs. She obviously removed the mascara without the benefit of a mirror, because now it looks worse. The funny thing with her is mascara wasn't even necessary in the first place - she has the longest eyelashes I have ever seen on a female.

Father: "D1, go back again. You look like a raccoon."

D1: "I do not."

Father: "Here – look at yourself in the hall mirror. Do you really want to go out looking like that?"

D4: "Well, at least now they don't have to kill a goat to see if that stuff is safe. We know it didn't hurt my sister, the raccoon."

Father and D1 (together): "Who asked you?"

D4 returns to her reading. D1 heads back upstairs. Finally, they all appear in some semblance of acceptable attire and accessories. I ask D2 to knock her shins to make sure she has taken off the shin guards. We pile into the car for the short trip to the mall.

Father (sniffing the air): "Is someone wearing perfume? Oh, never mind…"

20. Makeup - Part B

September, Year 2

In the last chapter we looked ahead at what *might* happen when the girls begin to discover the wonders of makeup in their teen years. However, I thought it might be interesting to see what they currently think of the subject as they approach ages 10,10,10 and 7 respectively. The following is a series of <u>actual</u> interviews with my four lovely daughters.

* * *

Scene I: Father, D2 and D3

Father: "I was just wondering, what do you girls think of lipstick?"

D3: "I'm never wearing lipstick. It's icky and gross. At least, not on my lips."

Father *(confused)*: "If not on your lips, on what part of your body would you be willing to wear lipstick?"

D3: "I don't know, just not on my lips."

D2 *(chiming in)*: "I'm wearing my soccer uniform to my wedding."

Father: "What does that have to do with lipstick?"

D2: "I just thought you would want to know that so you won't be surprised."

I won't be surprised, but I guarantee her husband will be – unless she marries David Beckham's son.

Father: "And what do you two think of mascara?"

D2: That's something to do with car racing, right?

D3 starts laughing hysterically.

D2: "What?! What did I say?"

Father: "That's NASCAR, but good try. Mascara is something women use to make their eyelashes look longer."

D3: "I won't use it - my eyelashes are long enough. Besides, after a while you start to look like a hockey player."

Father *(a former ice hockey player)*: "And this is a bad thing? Next topic - Have you ever heard of 'base'?"

D2: "What's that for?"

Father: "Some women use it to hide freckles."

D2: "Why would anyone want to do that?"

Father: "Good – remember that."

Point of explanation: D2 was born with one very unusual feature – she has a sprinkling of freckles on only the right side of her face. D1 has a few as well, but balanced on both sides, and D3 has none. We tell D2 they ran out in the middle. In any event, neither my wife nor I have ever seen anything like this before, and we think it's cute. Right now D2 thinks it's cute too – we hope that continues indefinitely.

Father: "What about earrings?"

D2 and D3 *(in unison)*: "No way!"

* * *

Scene II: Father and D1

Father: "I was just wondering, what do you think of lipstick?"

D1: "Lipstick – YUK!!! Why would you want to put that stuff on your lips?"

Father: "I wouldn't, and it sounds like you feel the same way. How about mascara?"

D1: "Like Jeff Gordon?"

Father: "Not NASCAR, mascara. You girls spend too much time watching ESPN."

This is uncanny, and a bit ironic as well. If you look at Jeff Gordon's #24 car, you will see that his main sponsor is

DuPont, one of whose key products is a series of performance coatings for automobiles. In a way, one could think of makeup as a different kind of performance coating. Perhaps there is a cross-marketing opportunity they need to explore.

Father: "What do you think of earrings?"

D1: "Why would I want to put holes in my ears and have stuff weigh my head down? Besides, they shoot you in the ear with a gun. What if they miss and put a hole in my head?"

That's pretty inescapable logic from a 10 year old.

Father: "And eye shadow?"

D1: "Looks stupid. Forget it."

* * *

Scene III: Father and D4 (our resident 7 year old fashion model)

Father: "I was just wondering, what do you think of lipstick?"

D4 *(breaks into a smile)*: "Yummy!"

Father: "What if it's the kind that doesn't taste like anything?"

I'll bet you didn't think I would know that!

D4: "It still looks good."

Father: "OK, how about mascara?"

D4: "It looks like it would itch."

Father: "Aren't you going to say something about car racing?"

D4 *(raises an eyebrow)*: "Now what does mascara have to do with car racing?"

Father: "You need to spend more time watching ESPN. Do you want to get earrings?"

D4: "Why would I want to put holes in my ears and have stuff weigh my head down? Besides, they shoot you in the ear with a gun. What if they miss and put a hole in my head?"

Father: "Did D1 tell you that?"

D4: "Of course."

Father: "One more question – do you like eye shadow?"

D4 *(batting her very large blue eyes)*: "I think my eyes look perfect just the way they are – don't you?"

Tough to argue with that one. I'm going to put this in a safe place for a few years and drag it out for the girls as they get ready to go to the mall.

21. Birth Month

October, Year 2

October is "Birth Month" around here. Between my siblings and me, seven of our nine collective offspring were born in October (I know what you are thinking about January...chuckle). With my daughters' four birthdays occurring within three days, there is really no way around the fact that this causes an especially big production in The Garden of Estrogen. My beloved, with her penchant for organization without peer, outdoes herself every year. Preparations begin during the summer as she selects the themes for the two parties (D1, D2 and D3 have one party, while D4 has her own). My wife is very good at finding inexpensive decorations to go with the themes, but she spends so much time finding them that sometimes I wonder if it wouldn't be cheaper just to pay up. Naturally, in the midst of all this preliminary activity, I wisely keep such thoughts to myself.

After school starts in September, the guest lists and dates are picked, taking into account current classmates, soccer teammates and schedules, religious holidays, etc. Unfortunately, D1, D2, and D3 now play on three *different* travel soccer teams. Consequently either a) the invite strategy is going to be a lot more challenging going forward, b) we will add one or two more parties, or c) we may need a bigger house. Of course in addition to the parties that take place *in* our house, there are also the four individual classroom parties to be planned (25 cupcakes apiece, plus napkins and plates).

During this flurry of preparation, the four lovely young girls in my life seem to be of the opinion that my business travel schedule needs to accommodate "Birth Month." In other words, the announcement of any trip that takes place during the very active period between my annual September London conference and November 1 is met by a state of shock. *Uh, excuse me little people, anyone else have any ideas about how to pay for things around here?* My wife, of course, understands, although last year when a week long business trip to Copenhagen culminated with my return the day of Party #1, she was a little suspicious of the timing. At least the flight arrived on schedule.

Not to be left out of the mix are the individual "Birth Week" privileges, which essentially constitutes getting to pick the menu for one dinner during the week. Predictably one child's favorite may head up the list of "can't stand it" for another, which effectively doubles the work on the nights in question.

On the evening of the big party (a sleepover for the past few years), my job is to get home early enough to get the little one out of the way for a few hours. We have a tradition of Daddy/D4 night at the local pizza joint and/or the mall, which seems to work well.

Meanwhile, the party proceeds with games, home-made pizza, birthday cake, and finally video with popcorn. D4 and I arrive home during the video, which gives me time to get her ready for bed. Next all the partygoers do the same, which triggers the "big negotiation":

- "I want to sleep next to _____."
- "You slept next to her last time."
- "How about _____ sleeps in the middle – that way she has two sides.
- "Does D4 have to join us?" *D4 anticipates this, and considering that possession is nine tenths of owner-ship, the fact that she is already in position with her sleeping bag and teddy bear goes a long way toward settling the issue.*
- "I don't like sleeping on the end – I'm scared."
- "I'm too hot in the middle." *One would think they could work out a solution to this one together with the previous point.*
- "If I sleep there my face will be next to your feet."
- "I want to sleep on the big stuffed Mickey Mouse. You take Tigger."
- "I want the light on."
- "I want the light off."
- And so on…

During this period, my wife and I are trying to put the kitchen and family room back in order so that we will be able to cook breakfast and find the furniture in the morning.

As the negotiation winds down, it is time for "Daddy's Awesome Bedtime Story" - my job exclusively. I have always found bedtime stories to be a bit of a paradox. On one hand, the story needs to be interesting enough that the audience wants to listen. On the other hand, they are supposed to fall asleep. It's a delicate balance, but I digress. One way or another, we end up with a dozen quiet little girls in their sleeping bags on the playroom floor, clutching their stuffed animals, worn out from the effects of the evening. I am thankful that 9 year old females seem as yet pretty much uninterested in talking about boys. Possibly because of the lack of this extra conversation stimulus, the girls drop off to sleep rather quickly – can they please stay this age?

Of course, no matter what the configuration resulting from the aforementioned negotiation, there is always some conscious or subconscious shifting of bodies so that the room ends up looking like a scene from *101 Dalmatians*. Sometimes my wife and I will just stand there and marvel at the sight before heading up to bed ourselves.

The highlight of the next morning's festivities (not including the breakfast free-for-all) is the "grand sorting of the clothes," as each girl tries to figure out which articles are hers. The object is to finish this activity before our foyer fills up with parents. Invariably we end up with a collection of clothes and accessories which remain unclaimed despite our ongoing efforts to locate their origin (note – does anyone know someone who is missing a West Point sweatshirt? Anyone want one?)

Compared to Party #1, the rest of the "Birth Month" sequence is a bit easier. D4's party has not yet progressed to a sleepover, and the hardest part of the subsequent "all-cousins" party is picking the date.

Of course, lurking at the very end of the month, with its own preparation extravaganza, is Halloween. Be afraid. Be very afraid...

22. Mixed Siblings

November, Year 2

I think kids who are reared in mixed sibling house-holds have an advantage over single sex siblings as they emerge from childhood. Close proximity and daily interaction eliminate at least some of the mystery about members of the opposite gender, even for someone like me who admittedly spent most of my time with my brother. Those of us who grew up this way certainly do not gain anywhere near a 100% understanding of our counterparts (which would leave me nothing to write about), but at least we nail down a few of the basics. For example, as a result of cohabitating with our sister, my brother and I reached college armed with some fundamental knowledge, including the following:

- We learned to communicate with the outside world using something other than the telephone, which was never available.
- Beginning at about age 12, for a few days each month, girls find their brothers <u>even more</u> annoying than usual.
- Baby oil trumps non-skid shower mat.

- 15 amp circuit plus 2000 Watt blow dryer at 110V = darkness.
- Don't bother getting into the bathroom when needed. Advance planning is crucial.

On the other hand, my sister also gained valuable information:

- Boys are slobs. If you are lucky, we <u>might</u> grow out of it in time to benefit your future sister in-law.
- Look before you sit down. The seat might be up.
- No, we're not killing each other. That's just how we play.
- We really don't care which outfit looks better on Barbie. And Ken is a wimp.

So, as the father of four girls, I have a dilemma. At this point there is no expectation of a brother in their future, which means my daughters will leave my care missing some critical life preparation. So I have to find ways to level the playing field vs. their peers who have brothers. Therefore, here is a sample of my all-girl child rearing strategy designed to produce confident, successful women.

<u>Challenge #1</u>: *Men and women don't communicate.*

<u>Reason</u>: There are three things to talk about – guy stuff, girl stuff and neutral stuff. For a lot of couples, this means they only have one third common ground for discussion.

<u>Solution</u>: Teach my daughters to talk "guy." No, I'm not instructing them in the fine art of swearing. The

school bus appears to be the venue for that education. I'm talking about sports, and I began as early as possible. When the triplets were infants I regularly lined them up in their bouncy seats to watch the New York Rangers play hockey on TV. Right after "mama" and "dada", they learned "Gretzky," "Messier," and "Leetch." However, I may have set them up for future therapy the day the Rangers scored a particularly exciting playoff overtime goal and my elated reaction freaked out all three of them.

Benefit: My kids are becoming sports nuts – soccer, basketball, swimming, baseball, etc. They even love NASCAR (especially Jeff Gordon).

Unintended Consequence: All of the women in my house think Derek Jeter is cute in spite of being Mets fans!

Challenge #2: *Girls routinely underperform boys in math.*

Reason: Not sure, but *Sports Illustrated* conducted a study that determined a correlation between time spent on sports and computational skills.

Solution: Same as Challenge #1.

Benefit: They are doing quite well in math.

Unintended Consequence: They don't seem to spell any better than I did at their age.

Challenge #3: *Little boys are disgusting, and my girls are not used to it.*

<u>Reason</u>: That's the way young males are – it's in our DNA. Get used to it!

<u>Solution</u>: None – I like my girls just the way their DNA is programmed.

<u>Unintended Consequence</u>: Some of their little girl friends taught them how to burp on demand. I'm not exactly sure how to react to this, except to make sure they are not holding a beer.

At the risk of being redundant, let me stress that I'm not trying to produce boys here. Rather, I'm hoping to end up with four confident females who will have enough common ground with males despite the circumstances of their childhood. Furthermore, in the distant future are dating and marriage, so creating a bunch of masculine or gender-confused girls would be somewhat counterproductive. Fortunately, my wife is doing a great job on the "girl" side, so no worries there.

<u>Progress Report</u>: So far so good as they reach 10, 10, 10 and 7 respectively. One weekend last fall as the kids finished getting ready for worship services, I stood at the bottom of the stairs and looked up to see four lovely girls decked out in dresses, hair done, and even wearing some jewelry. Of course I'm biased, but it took my breath away to see it. However, as we were running typically late, my reverie had to be short-lived. I called up to them, "Wow! You all look so beautiful. We're late - come on downstairs. Big three, have you set out your soccer gear? You have early games this afternoon and there will be almost no time to change after services."

As if choreographed, the three of them simultaneously raised their dresses to reveal their soccer uniforms underneath. In unison they replied, "All set, Dad. Let's go!"

That's my girls!

23. My Dad's Fault

December, Year 2

Some people spend the better part of their adult lives trying to understand how they arrived at a certain point. Soul searching, religion, mind altering substances, thousands of dollars in therapy, all leading to the same inescapable conclusion: it's our parents' fault.

I can say with absolute certainty and without resorting to any of the abovementioned methods that my status as "The Gardener" is entirely my father's fault (my mom, of course, is blameless). Wait – I can hear what you are thinking. "So you have a wife and four daughters. Big deal! Lots of people have only daughters – remember the Sheikh of Midian (Exodus 2:16)? He had seven." Ah yes, but how many people do you know who have had, not one, but all of the following experiences:

- "House Dad" to 100 daughters in a college sorority
- Coached various sports for women ranging in ages from 5 to 45

- Work in an office with almost all women
- Triplet daughters plus one more

You have to admit, it's a little unusual. I am a veritable expert on women, which means that I have learned that I know nothing about them. And neither do you – unless you are, in fact, a woman – in which case you just <u>might</u> know something.

As you can see, my wife and four daughters represent but a single step in a sequence of nearly constant estrogen immersion that began with a single event. But first, a little background...

I remember that when I was a kid my father used to talk about the balance that exists in nature. If one part goes out of whack, there is bound to be a reaction. Fortunately, nature is fairly resilient. It takes a real shock to the system to create a reaction of any magnitude – one which my father inadvertently caused.

Now my dad was definitely "all guy" - one of three brothers, son of a U.S. Marine, and always in need of a shave. OK, so he was also a PhD with an IQ that was so high it was off the charts, but even when he was doing geek stuff it was cool - like creating some of the first color videotape technology, working on missile guidance systems, or designing giant furnaces. Dad built his own house from the ground up. He could work with his hands equally well on wood, fabric or steel, and had a physical strength that belied his wiry frame. He was also a true gentleman in every sense of the word.

So what did my "man's man" of a father do to set me on this path? The critical moment occurred early on when my wife and I were dating. She suggested in his presence that I would look good in a pink shirt. My dad immediately transfixed her with one of his classic stares - his blue/gray eyes could burn a hole through a person even when he was amused – and emphatically declared, "Staffin men do <u>not</u> wear pink. They do <u>not</u> mince; they do <u>not</u> puree; they do <u>not</u> eat quiche (egg pies yes, quiche no)." My beloved, only about 20 years old at the time, was positively mortified. Even when she discovered that his feigned shock was a little fun at her expense, she also realized that he was quite serious about men not wearing anything pink.

What my father evidently did not realize was that the rules of Nature had changed (I think it happened sometime in the late 60's). Men are now required to be in touch with their sensitive side. Lightning flashed. Thunder rolled. The natural imbalance had been created.

My younger brother, who tends to be a little more rebellious than I, has been known to sport a pink shirt on rare occasion (and, as he has the physical attributes of a typical NFL defensive back, he can wear pretty much whatever he wants). He is an excellent cook, so I'll bet he even has cause to mince or puree when the situation dictates. He has two sons and one daughter: equilibrium for him.

By contrast, I think pink looks fine on little girls, but I have never felt even slightly compelled to choose that color for myself. I can't remember ever mincing or pureeing. But shortly after my father's emphatic declaration, I found myself assistant coaching an all-women's ice hockey team. Then followed the sorority house-dad experience, the four daughters, etc. In a word, *payback.*

Don't get me wrong – I'm not unhappy with this turn of events, and I would not trade my experiences for anyone else's. But as Dad would have said, nature always manages to balance itself out in the end.

* * *

Author's Note: Dr. Robert Staffin passed away nearly five years before the first Postcard was written. Anyone who had the good fortune to know him was better for the experience.

YEAR 3 - AGES 10, 10, 10 AND 7

24. Slammed Doors

January, Year 3

*** *Warning – this one is a bit strange, even for me.* ***

I wonder how the practice of slamming doors evolved, and why is it a predominantly female practice? I'm pretty sure it's not something you see very often in nature. Let's take a quick look around the animal kingdom and then analyze the results:

Butterfly Father: "Listen to me, young lady. You are not going out with those wings on – you're too young."
Butterfly Daughter: "I'm going back into my cocoon and not coming out." *SLAM!!! Patter patter patter.*
Father: "Now look what you did – you knocked all the other cocoons off the tree."

Beaver Father: "Young lady, did you get your tail pierced?"
Beaver Daughter: "All the girls at school are doing it."
Father: "Go back to the lodge and take that thing out."

Daughter (grabs the nearest log): *SLAM!!! Disappears into her room in the lodge.*
Father: "You just ruined my dam, dammit! – there goes the whole lake right down the stream."

Spider Father: "Young lady, you had better be planning to eat that dragon fly you just caught."
Spider Daughter: "But he's so cute."
Father: "Go back to the web. I'm eating this one myself."
Daughter: *RIPPP!!!! (web is now in tatters)*
Father: "I will not stand for this behavior, Charlotte! I want you to spin a web 25 times saying 'It's not a dinner date, it's dinner.' And don't be careless with your spelling. Last time when you wrote the shopping web for mom and she wanted some figs, you wrote "Some Pig" by mistake. Now everyone on the farm thinks you are a genius, and no one around here can make a BLT."

* * *

Since none of the above scenarios are likely, I would have to conclude that although we are basically animals, slamming doors is an unavoidably human trait.

But here is where the gender divergence comes in. I think it's basically the lack of an appropriate release mechanism. Men have ESPN and Clint Eastwood movies (or toy soldiers when they are younger). After watching four college football games and Dirty Harry, what motive could there possibly be to slam a door? And if a guy really goes over the edge, a beer can in the forehead (which I have yet to try) or finding a convenient full contact football or hockey game (frequently, at least in my younger days) is a much more beneficial outlet. Uncivilized? Perhaps, but a frustration vent nevertheless. On the other hand, after watching your little sister mess up all of your stuff for the fourth time this week and being told you can't wear "that shirt" out of the house, don't you think there is an explosion just waiting to happen? Elementary, my dear Watson.

I live with five women. What should I do? Teach them to play ice hockey? Too expensive. Soccer apparently isn't crazy enough (which is actually a good thing). So I look to the ultimate source of inspiration from my childhood, my father (who is undoubtedly looking down from above and laughing at me). When my sister started slamming doors, my father did two things. First, he managed to rig the bathroom door so it could not be slammed. This undoubtedly saved my brother and me from losing a few fingers as my sister hit adolescence in a house with only one bathroom. Second, he imposed a 25 cent fine for slamming doors. My sister, whose many positive qualities include being a good saver, immediately saw the wisdom of changing her ways.

While I have only been able to render one of our 2.5 bathroom doors slam-proof, the monetary fine has recently been introduced with somewhat satisfactory results. The door slamming has diminished, and the little one still has all her fingers, which is good. However, occasionally we still get some interesting exchanges:

D3: "D4, have you been in my stuff again? Everything is messed up, and now I have to clean it."

D4: "I was looking for a soccer shirt and socks."

D3: "Get out!" *Closes the door hard.*

Father *(trying to decide if a threshold has been crossed)*: "Was that a door slam I just heard?"

D2 *(our own thrifty one)*: "Come on, Dad. For 25 cents she should be allowed to slam the door way harder than that."

If this doesn't work over the long term, I'm installing revolving doors in every room of the house.

25. Adam and Eve

February - Valentine's Day, Year 3

As we know, the collection of books we call the Bible can be quite detailed on certain topics, and extremely sketchy on others. For example, the account of Jacob and Rachel's Valentine's Day experience (Chapter 2) was actually found in a set of scrolls unearthed in 1964. The writings, entitled *The Jacob Memoirs: Oy, I Married Too Many!* contained a much expanded account of the life of Jacob and his large family that, among other things, helped Andrew Lloyd Weber and Tim Rice fill in the missing pieces for the musical *Joseph and the Amazing Technicolor Dreamcoat*.

Similarly, the book of Genesis is quite brief when it comes to the life of Adam and Eve in Eden. The entire story takes up a fraction of a page. Most of what we know about the true First Couple really comes from Adam's autobiography entitled: *Why Couldn't It Have Been a Kumquat?*

You may be surprised to know that Cain and Abel weren't the first two children. The Bible tends not to focus on females unless they do something really good (Esther, Ruth), really bad (Delilah), or provide subject matter for the Oprah book list (Dinah – *The Red Tent*).

According to Adam's aforementioned autobiography, he and Eve produced four offspring – all girls – while still residing in Eden. Cain and Abel came much later.

* * *

The Setting: Eden – Valentine's Day, 5760+ years ago

Eve: "Hi, honey. You're home a bit late tonight."

Adam: "Yes, tough day at the office."

Eve: "You work in paradise?"

Adam: "Of course. The rent on this garden is astronomical. You know, even He has to pay real estate taxes. And what do you think I do all day, play golf?"

Eve: "What's golf?"

Adam (*quickly*): "Never mind."

Eve: "So what exactly do you do at the office?"

Adam: "I name animals. Only a few animals are explicitly named in the Book of Genesis, so it's my job to name the rest. I observe them and try to match their names with their personalities."

Eve: "Like what?"

Adam: "Well, take the various cats for instance. There's this big shaggy one that sunbathes all day while his wife does all the work. His wife calls him a *Lyin'good-for-nothing* which seems fine to me. I just shortened it to *Lion*. Of course, his wife wasn't too pleased when she realized that was her name as well."

Eve: "You think?"

Adam: "My boss was pretty happy, though. Apparently He plans to use my new name in a story He is planning for some guy named Isaiah, and He says lion sounds a lot better with lamb, fatling, etc. than 'big hairy yellow cat'."

Eve: "Tell me more. You know I love to hear you talk shop."

Adam: "Just the other day, I was playing cards with a spotted cat – pretty big, can run like the wind. Anyway, I caught him hiding an ace of spades in a hairball."

Eve: "What did you name him?"

Adam: "Cheetah." (*saw that one coming a mile away*)

Eve: "No more cats. How did you come up with the one who calls himself *elephant*?"

Adam: "Purely by accident. I took one look at him and meant to say 'Hell-of-a-giant mouse!' Unfortunately, I sneezed at an inopportune time and what came out of my mouth just stuck. To make matters worse, now the elephant is actually afraid of the mouse."

Eve: "That whole sneeze thing is a visual I didn't need. And that poor ape-looking animal that has been so depressed - what did you do to him?"

Adam: "Similar situation. I was remarking on his coloring, 'Aren't you tan,' but I had a mouth full of those cookies the girls baked for me. I guess it got a bit garbled. Too bad for Mr. Orangutan, eh?"

Eve: "That seems a bit haphazard if you ask me. Hope you are not planning on a raise any time soon. And now I have to ask – what about the woodpecker and the shi-tzu?"

Adam: "Don't even go there. The kids might read this someday."

Eve: "Enough about work. You're starting to make my head spin. What do you have planned for the evening?"

Adam: "I thought perhaps we could go bowling."

Eve: "Where is there a bowling alley in Eden? Did they put one in next to the Starbucks?"

Adam: "There isn't one. We find a palm tree, look for a fallen coconut and use that."

Eve: "And pins?"

Adam: "There are no pins. Normally I just roll the coconut down the path, and He calls to me and tells me what my score would have been. I even have this cool looking thing called a *bowling shirt*, only I'm not sure what you do with it since we are all naked. I use it to wipe off the coconut ball."

Eve: "Sounds pretty lame to me. When do you do all this bowling?"

Adam: "On guys' night out."

Eve: "But we have four daughters. There are no guys except you."

Adam: "A minor difficulty, I admit."

Eve: "We need to get you some sons!"

Adam: "OK, forget bowling. Would you like to see my fig leaf collection?"

Eve: "You collect fig leaves? What on earth would you do with them?"

Adam: "Sure I collect them. We don't have baseball cards yet (when they do I want to get the Methuselah rookie card – in about 900 years it could be a rare commodity). Those fig leaves could be worth something too someday. Think how much they'll fetch on e-Bay.

Eve: "Well, ipskay the igleafay for now, udstay."

Adam: "What was that gibberish?"

Eve: "It's called Pig Latin. The girls taught it to me."

Adam: "Pig Latin you say? I heard some round pink-ish colored animals talking like that this morning. 'Pig' sounds perfect for a name, don't you think?"

Eve *(smiling coyly)*: "Back to tonight. What say we start getting you those sons?"

Adam: "Sounds super. Let's just stay in. You put the girls to bed, I'll run down to Blockbuster. There is a new futuristic film by somebody named Mel Brooks called *History of the World, Part I*. I want to see what is going to happen to us."

Eve: "Great. Oh, by the way, I bought you an extra special dessert for later."

Adam: "Can't wait."

Two hours later – the children are finally asleep and Adam and Eve are sitting on the living room couch.

Eve: "Well, that was disappointing. We never got to see the movie, and it took forever to get the girls in bed."

Adam: "How was I supposed to know we needed a tape player? I never even heard of a Sony Betamax. Do you think we should try to buy one or wait for some newer technology? Anyway, at least your dessert was as good as advertised. What was it, any-way?"

Eve: "It's called Apple Crisp."

Adam *(horrified)*: "YOU DIDN'T!!!"

Eve: "What? A snake oil sales rep came to the door this afternoon – a really funny looking creature. He was actually out of snake oil (go figure), but he had this great tasting dessert. He said you would think I was very smart for buying it."

Adam: "I think you just cost me a bowling score-keeper. He is not going to like this at all."

Eve: "I've got an idea. Let's go back and check out your fig leaf collection again."

26. Mealtime – Part A

March, Year 3

Perhaps my memory is faulty, but I seem to recall that the family on The Waltons used to sit down to dinner together in a reasonably organized way. Same for the Brady Bunch (although the "Marcia, Marcia, Marcia" stuff had to grate on the rest of the group).

By contrast, dinner has always been a fairly crazy event around our house. Scratch that. All meals are a bit crazy, but dinner even more so, beginning the very first day we brought the trio home.

Date: October 12, Ten Years Ago
Place: Basking Ridge, NJ
Scene: The triplets, only four days old, have arrived home at our townhouse for the first time. The parents of my beloved Queen have come along to help us get the babies settled. After much videotaping and unpacking, the kids are asleep in their bassinets.

Grandmother: "Do you want us to stay for a while?"

Mother (*eager to begin parenthood at home despite being only four days removed from a C-section*): "No Mom, you

---

and Dad have been so much help already, we can take it from here."

Grandmother: "Are you sure?"

Grandfather: "OK, let's go."

Hugs and kisses. The grandparents depart. My wife and I stand over the bassinets and marvel at three sleeping babies.

Father: "Isn't D1 cute?"

Mother: "That's not D1, that's D2. Look at the hospital band on her ankle."

Father: "Oops. Oh well."

Mother: "Hey, D3 is waking up."

Father: "So are D1 and D2."

Babies suddenly begin crying in unison. I spring into action and do what any brand new father would do in such a circumstance: run to the front door to see if the grandparents are still in the parking lot. No luck.

Mother: "I think they are hungry. There's some baby formula in that bag of stuff they gave us at the hospital."

Note: For those who may not have done the math, it may come as a surprise to learn that the female body is anatomically mismatched to a set of triplets. Having had nearly 8 months to determine with near certainty that two does not equal three, we prepared ourselves for the inescapable fact that feeding the trio would be a combination of nursing-plus-bottle in our house.

Father *(rummaging through duffel bag)*: "I found it. Now we need to figure out what to do. In the hospital they just handed me a bottle of that sugar water stuff, and we were good to go. Wow, look at all these instructions. Did you know we need to sterilize a whole bunch of things? And then we need to heat up more water to warm the bottle. This could take a while."

Several minutes pass. Babies cry louder.

Mother *(calling into the kitchen from the couch)*: "How are you doing in there?"

Father: "Not good. I can't seem to figure out what gets sterilized, the formula or the bottles."

Mother: "We have five college degrees between us. It shouldn't be that hard. Read the instructions out loud."

Father: "I've got a better idea."

I dial the phone number of my in-laws – not only do they have five college degrees between them as well, but more importantly, they are experienced parents. They have just arrived home, and were apparently expecting the call. The Queen Mother patiently explains that the formula is ready-to-drink right out of the can. All I need to do is grab one of the brand new bottles we got at the hospital. Open the can. Fill a bottle. Attach the nipple and the top. Repeat two more times. Warm the bottles on the stove in a small pot of water. Test the temperature. Feed the babies. Then put the unused portion in the refrigerator. When the bottle is empty, separate the components and put them in the dishwasher. WOW! That wasn't so bad.

* * *

In the ensuing weeks we began to refer to meals as "feeding frenzies." The routine consisted of trying to change three little ones, nurse one (my wife's job, of course), feed two, and get them back in the cribs so we could get some sleep. My wife even managed to do a lot of this alone when I headed back to work, although The Queen Mother seemed to always know when my wife needed a little help.

Notwithstanding the rather rocky start, I did master the art of mixing formula from concentrate. Eventually the girls were collectively consuming a gallon of the stuff every 36 hours (in addition to nursing). When they finally switched to regular milk our grocery bill dropped by about $9 per day!

Note: D4 never drank from a bottle. In fact, once my wife explained to me that I didn't need to immerse her in warm water before each feeding, things went very smoothly for all involved.

Returning to the triplets, solid food brought another set of challenges. The new procedure involved setting out a large waterproof tablecloth on the dining room carpet of our townhouse (the kitchen was far too small), upon which sat three booster seats. We would open up several of the myriad of baby food jars with some kind of pureed fruit or vegetable and try to get more inside the children than on the wall. It was not a

---

rare occurrence for me to arrive home from work in the midst of one of these events to find my wife and the floor similarly covered with baby food. At such point she would exclaim, "Look at what *your* children did!" hand me a spoon, and head upstairs for a few moments of welcome solitude.

Finally, after about a year we moved to our present house, which has a real eat-in kitchen. We could at last use regular high chairs and line the trio up along the wall facing the table. By then the girls could feed themselves after a fashion, and if I was home from work early enough it was my job to serve and entertain them while they ate - dinner theater, Staffin style. Unfortunately, my repertoire was limited (how many times can you ask "And what sound does a sheep make?") Naturally, I turned to sports. I soon had them memorizing the hand signals used by American football referees. It's really funny to hear three toddlers try to say "illegal procedure" while rolling their arms. For those of you who have watched a lot of American football, what was somewhat less funny was when the signal for "incomplete pass" resulted in knocking food off a neighboring tray.

During the whole time the kids were very small (and with the arrival of D4 on the scene), my wife and I didn't attempt to eat dinner together with the girls except on rare occasions. It was just too wearing, and we ended up with stomach aches.

As the girls have gotten older, we have tried to establish family dinners on a regular basis. But there are some real challenges. The natural inclination of children at this age (10 and 7) seems to be to race through their food. The lone exception is D1, who tends to be blissfully unaware of the passage of time – this creates a different problem at what is supposed to be the end of the meal. The net result of all this lack of synchronization is that we have several kids finishing what is on their plates just as my wife and I sit down, which makes us feel like a pair of yo-yos:

- "More milk, please."
- "Can I have my fruit now?"
- "I spilled."
- "D3 took the butter and won't give it back."
- "I'm still hungry – are there seconds?"
- "Mmbgmb blthbm ergblg." *I have no idea what that means – D2 had food in her mouth when she said it.*

By the time we have poured, served, sponged, adjudicated, and served again, our food is cold. The solution we seem to have arrived at to prevent such an occurrence is to make sure that everyone is seated before the meal, and of course no one starts eating before saying grace as a family. The kids can even get their own drinks from the refrigerator, which has been helpful – except for the day that D3 dropped a full gallon jug of milk on the floor, causing the container to burst and the milk to seemingly cover the entire kitchen.

On the whole, our system is a success. Now if I can only get the kids to speak slowly and one at a time, I might be able to eat and simultaneously decode what these four females are actually saying... or not.

27. Mealtime - Part B

April, Year 3

Last chapter we had a look at the evolution of meal time in the Garden of Estrogen. Now let's listen in on an actual dinner conversation.

* * *

I have a confession. When I'm alone with the kids at dinner time, I don't even bother to try to eat. I just accept my role as waiter. Once the table has been cleared and the kids are in bed, I prepare a plate of something and catch up on work e-mails, or sit down in front of a baseball or hockey game. During the meal, however, I try to pay attention to the dinner conversation, which has become rather interesting of late (and the excuse for this Postcard).

The Scene: Dinner at the Staffin house. Mother is out for the evening. Father is in charge.

Father: "How was soccer practice?"

D1: "A, B, C, D..."

Father: "I said how was soccer practice?"

D3: "Good dad. Wait one minute."

D1: "...E, F, G, H, I, J, K"

D2: "Stop!"

D1: "A, B, C, D"

D2: "Stop!"

D3: "K.D. - Kyle Davis."

D1, D4 *(in unison)*: "Ooooh!"

Father: "I don't get it."

D3: "D2 is going to marry Kyle Davis."

Father: "Who is Kyle Davis?"

D3: "A boy."

Father: "Oh, that's good. I thought he might have been a platypus."

D4: "What's a platypus?"

Father: "A mammal that answers to the name "Kyle Davis."

D1, D2, D3 *(in unison)*: "Daaaaaadddy!"

Father: "So who's Kyle Davis?"

D3: "A boy in my class. D2 is going to marry him."

Father (taking this surprise betrothal in stride): "Does he know?"

D2: "Of course not. It's whatever letters you stop on. It was K and D."

I don't remember conversations like this with my brother, so I pour D1 more milk and keep listening.

D1: "D4 kissed a boy, you know."

Father: "D4 is only seven. When did this happen?"

D1: "In preschool, three years ago."

At this point it seems like a good idea to go empty the dishwasher.

D3 (calling from the table): "What hand do I cut my food with?"

Father (happy for the change of subject): "The right hand."

D3: "That means I use my left brain."

I didn't know they knew that. Score one for their elementary school.

D2: "And that means you are holding the fork with your left hand and using your right brain."

Father: "Correct."

D1: "Look, I'm using my left brain." *She waves her right hand.*

D2: "And I'm using my right brain." *Waves her left hand.*

At this point, I'm feeling back on safe ground, when suddenly D4 decides to make an observation.

D4: "Let's see, left brain," (*wiggles fingers on right hand*), "right brain" (*wiggles left hand*). *Next, she looks straight down at her lap.* "Hmm, right in the middle. I wonder which part of the brain controls down there."

Uh oh.

D3: "And how about boys? What part of the brain controls <u>that</u>?"

Saw that one coming. Of course, women have claimed for centuries that when it comes to "that," the mental control is frequently exerted in the exact opposite direction.

Nevertheless, as I was and still am at a complete loss for words in answering either D3 or D4, I must borrow from Mark Twain's narrative concerning an equally embarrassing moment in Tom Sawyer - "We will now close a curtain of charity on the scene."

28. The Expectant Father

May/June, Year 3

Mother's Day and Father's Day take on a whole new meaning when you have children. Sure, we still need to remember to call our parents, but now the holiday is about US!

* * *

Because The Queen and I started down the path of parenthood with triplets, almost nothing about our experience nearly ten years ago could be considered normal. When D4 came along, we were in the midst of potty training D1, D2 and D3, so even that was a bit of a blur.

Nevertheless, I have an active imagination and have often wondered what life would have been like had there been more than one minute between the birth of our first child and the arrival of the second. And so, in honor of all the first time Dads (and Moms) out there, I have composed this "Ode to the Expectant Father."

* * *

The due date's just around the corner and I'm not sure I'm prepared,
In fact, if truth be told, I'm just a little more than scared.

I think back on the wild nights our early marriage had,
Until the E.P.T. turned blue and said "You'll be a dad."

Don't get me wrong, I'm very excited, but also quite uncertain.
I can't even remember little things like closing the shower curtain.

But the baby is coming, ready or not. It's time to pay the piper,
And as the day approaches I think "Can I really change a diaper?"

I know my wife will wake me in the middle of the night,
When I feel completely paralyzed by first time parent fright.

So I jump into my car and drive like Mario Andretti,
Just to make it to the hospital before the baby's ready.

Then I get to where I'm going, and I realize I'm alone,
I was so intent on getting there I left my wife at home.

So I barrel down the highway to pick up my better half,
But when I get inside the door all I can do is laugh.

The baby wasn't coming yet, my wife just wanted water,
By this time I was sure I'd know the answer – son or daughter?

So I climb back into bed and say "I won't be fooled, so there!"
But three hours later she wakes again and gasps "My suitcase – where?"

Only this time I roll over 'cause I think it's just a joke,
When a little voice beside my ear says "Hey, my water broke."

"Oh no," I yell, "It's really coming. Let's get out of here!"
My wife adds sweetly "Yes, and don't forget me this time, dear."

I check the house before we go, and everything is there,
The crib, the changing table, and a brand new teddy bear.

Down the highway once again, though this time it's for real,
Weaving in and out of cars with quite uncommon zeal.

We make it there in record time and then we have to wait,
It seems the OB-GYN is running a little late.

They prep my wife and give her stuff we hope will ease the pain,
Those early thoughts of natural childbirth long since down the drain.

The doc shows up, examines her, and says "The baby's ready,"
I wonder what I'm supposed to do - just stand and throw confetti?

Then I recall our childbirth classes. I'm here to coach and coax!
I also remember I promised my wife – no stupid delivery jokes.

Doctors, nurses, orderlies, around the room they swirl,
'Til we finally hear the newborn cry and doc says "It's a girl!"

The family arrives at the hospital and my brother says "Not bad.
A baby girl, you did it bro'. You're finally a Dad!"

29. Boyfriends – A Preview

July, Year 3

The big girls have now moved on from their elementary school (K-4) and will begin intermediate school this fall. The little one will be entering second grade, but she thinks she can keep up (and in many ways she does). It's an amazing in-between age, as the little girls start to fade and the pre-teens struggle to emerge. But before the little girls disappear entirely, I need to take a few snapshots for the time capsule. This month we take a close look at the subject of dating.

* * *

I don't know what worries me more:

- The idea that one day my daughters will have boyfriends.
- The idea that it may happen at approximately the same time (at least for the big three – this is NOT one area where I want the little one to play catch-up).

However, I remember how completely inept most boys are at all things social, so perhaps I still have some breathing room. Of course, one should not assume the topic doesn't enter their thought process, but for the time being I can still observe and be (mostly) amused.

Disclaimer: my daughters claim that I have muddled some of this account. If so, I take full responsibility for any misidentification of my daughters or misinterpretation that may have occurred. I was writing as quickly as I could, and 10 year old girls have a tendency to talk simultaneously (no, really?) Of course, any actual names that appear here have been changed.

The Scene: Dinner time at the Staffin house late spring – the girls are about to conclude their 4th grade experience.

The Queen has a speaking engagement, and I am alone with the kids. As we have learned, this means they eat while I serve and listen.

D3: "Kevin is so annoying. Daddy, why are boys so annoying?"

Father: "It's something we practice starting in pre-school. There is a special "annoying" class that only boys can attend where they teach us how to drive girls crazy. Then we spend a lifetime perfecting the techniques."

D4: "Really?"

D3: "No silly, you can always tell when Daddy is joking. He gets that look like he's about to smile."

D1: "Are you writing this down? Oh no, he's making a Postcard! Let's change the subject."

I think I'm going to have to change tactics one of these days. They are getting wise to my research methods.

D3 *(ignoring D1's warning)*: "Daddy, are you Mommy's boyfriend?"

Father: "Yes."

D4: "How can you be her boyfriend if you are married?"

Father: "You get married when you decide you want to be boyfriend and girlfriend forever. I take it none of you have boyfriends, right?"

D2: "D1 likes Mark'"

D1: "Eew, I do not. He curses."

D2: "D3 chases him."

D3: "He asked me to."

Father: "And so you do?"

D3: "Sure, why not?"

Why didn't I think of that when I was a teenager? She looks cute. "Hey, chase me. Want to go out on a date? Great!"

D1: "He thinks he is funny, but he is completely annoying."

D2: "Totally."

D3: "You know, boys think it's cool to have a girl-friend."

Father: "Why?"

D1 and D2 *(in unison):* "I have no idea."

D3: "I don't know, but it seems that way."

Father: "What do they do?"

D1: "They don't do anything. They just say they have a girlfriend and leave them alone."

Father: "So let me get this straight. Boys annoy you, right?"

D1: "Yes."

Father: "And then they leave you alone? This sounds like a good thing." *(especially for Dad)*

D1 and D2: "No, you don't get it."

D1: "They say they have a girlfriend, but they don't do anything. They don't give Valentines or go out on dates. They just leave the subject alone."

Father: "What if you ask the girl?"

D3: "The girls say 'No, I don't even talk to him!' or 'He's the most annoying person in the universe!' "

Father: "So the boys are making it up."

D1: "Yes. They just say it and go do boy things."

Father: "Has any boy said he likes you?"

D1 and D3: "No."

D2: "Well…"

D3 *(always the helpful one, whispers)*: "Jake."

Father: "Did Jake say he likes you?"

D2: "No, but I think he does."

Father: "And how does that make you feel?"

D2: "Bad."

D3: "I put ice down his back."

D1: "Yeah, she beats up the boys."

Father: "So, boys like D2, and then D3 beats them up."

D3: "I don't really beat them up. I just protect the girls – especially when boys steal their stuff."

D2: "It's <u>really</u> nice to have D3 on your side."

Note: D3 is only 10, but she is about to reach 5 feet tall and is as strong as some adults – a future power forward if she gets serious about basketball. If I were an annoying little boy, I think I would steer clear of D3's friends.

Now let's see what D4 thinks of all this. She has been listening to this whole conversation with a mixture of fascination and skepticism.

Father: "D4, what do you think about boyfriends?"

D4: "They're dumb. I want to marry a boy that doesn't like kissing."

Father: "Have you ever had a boyfriend?"

D4: "No."

Father: "When do you think you will have a boyfriend?"

D4: "College."

Father: "Good answer."

D4: "Or high school, whichever comes first."

D2: "Not such a good answer, eh Daddy?" *I don't know which is more scary – the thought of D4 dating or the fact that D2 is starting to find me predictable.*

D3: "You know what's cool? They have to ask me if I want to be their girlfriend. And I can say no whenever I want."

Father: "What if they don't ask?"

D3: "I'll ask them." *At least I'm raising a modern woman...*

D3: "Or else I'll hypnotize them." *...and apparently a mystic as well.*

D2: "Or better yet, ask them just before they are about to go to sleep when they are really tired."

Father: "You aren't going to be anywhere near where boys are going to sleep."

D3: "Sure we are. In college. You just walk into their room when they are lying in bed and scream 'ASK ME!!!'"

You have to give D3 points for originality there. I attended four years of undergrad and two years of graduate school and never heard of anything like that. Not sure if my girls are typical in the way they look at this whole boyfriend thing at this age (aside from the screaming in the dorm room tactic), but it will be fascinating to see how this all resolves itself over the next decade.

30. Sleep

August/September, Year 3

The Queen and I were recently having lunch together – just the two of us. She popped open a Snapple Iced Tea and looked at the cap to read one of the "fun facts" that are printed on the underside. According to the Snapple folks, the average elephant sleeps only two hours each night. Upon reading this, The Queen observed, "Well, that makes at least one other mammal who knows what it is like to constantly have their sleep truncated."

I thought it was funny.

* * *

Before we had children, The Queen and I had a fairly standard routine. We would frequently find ourselves short on sleep during the week, as the demands of our respective jobs and my late night ice hockey league took their toll. On at least one of the weekend days, however, we would catch up by sleeping until noon. Football Sundays were the best, as we would roll out of bed, catch the last few minutes of one of the Sunday talk shows, and watch the NFL pregame over brunch.

For the two years that we were house parents in Delta Delta Delta Sorority at Cornell, the routine was not that different, except that when the Sunday morning bagel/donut delivery truck would pass under our window and wake me up at 6:00 am, I would throw on a pair of sweats, run out to the front hall, snag two blueberry muffins (for me) and a double chocolate donut (for the Queen), and go back to bed for about five more hours.

* * *

Babies change everything, and having three babies REALLY changes everything. The triplets were on a two-and-a-half hour cycle, which meant that after changing and feeding three of them, we had about 60-90 minutes to sleep - if we were lucky. At least they were somewhat synchronized, which is probably the reason I am still sane enough to operate a word processor all these years later. Nevertheless, the resulting sleep deprivation got to the point where one night The Queen woke me up frantically, yelling, "There's a baby on the dresser!"

As I stared, bleary eyed, across the darkened room, it looked like she was right. I leapt out of bed, crossed to the dresser and scooped up the 'baby' – which turned out to be a crumpled sweatshirt. "Honey, we *really* need more sleep!"

And as The Queen is quick to remind me when I relate the aforementioned incident, I would occasionally wake up patting the blankets to make sure I had not forgotten to put one of the babies back in the crib. Before you call the Child Services Hotline and report me, you should know that I never actually found a baby in the blankets - my record on successful returns-to-crib was a perfect 100%.

Finally, one weekend we decided we needed to find a way to catch up. We barely got out of bed for an entire day. The Queen and I each slept on opposite sides of our king mattress with the babies in between. When they woke, I changed them (only if they really needed it), stumbled to the bathroom to warm a bottle of ready-made formula in the sink, climbed back into bed, helped feed them, and passed out.

The first time the girls slept through the night was New Year's Eve, which was ironic considering we were the ones staying up most of the night with my parents. Nevertheless, it was a significant achievement at the time. From that point forward we were still sleep deprived due to lack of weekend catch-up, but at least we were functional. It also helped that The Queen's brother started showing up at our house most nights at about 11:00 pm to watch *Law and Order* and help feed the babies. I was able to get some extra work done, and The Queen got a few more hours of sleep so she could handle the early wake-up. Of course all these years later, if someone turns on *Law and Order* and the girls hear that "dong dong" chime, they run to the refrigerator to grab a glass of milk (just kidding, Pavlov).

One advantage of having all those miniature people in cribs was that we knew exactly where they were while we were in bed (hallucinations notwithstanding). Even when the girls moved from cribs to toddler beds, we put a gate across the door to their bedroom, so if they got out of bed they were still penned in. Many mornings we would find them asleep on the carpet near the gate.

Then came potty training. Suddenly we could not pen the girls in because they might need to use the bathroom in the middle of the night. We decided to start closing our bedroom door for privacy, which worked great until the first time we had a thunderstorm. The Queen and I were lying in bed enjoying (ahem!) the sound of the rain, when suddenly we heard a cry, followed by the patter of little feet getting closer, and then WHAM! Something hit the door – D2 as it turned out, running at full speed. Screaming child with bruised forehead trumps sound of rain and pretty much everything else.

The kids quickly figured out how to use the doorknob, which made for fewer bangs and bruises, but any time one of them got a little scared, we would wake up in the morning to find a child asleep on the floor next to the bed, curled up with a few teddy bears and a blanket. As Romeo observed in Chapter 14, it's amazing we ever managed to create D4!

31. Directions

October, Year 3

Several years ago my wife and I were walking through the town center of Naperville, Illinois. We were with another couple and our collective six daughters, trying to locate the restaurant at which we planned to eat dinner. As one might expect, herding all the children in the same direction was a challenge. Either the place wasn't quite where anyone remembered it, or perhaps it just seemed like a long walk with such a large entourage of little people in tow.

Dodging a sandwich board that advertised a Tarot reader, we made our way past a rather odd looking storefront, when suddenly a woman in a long flowing gown and way too much eye makeup burst through the door, walked up to me, and asked mysteriously, "Would you like me to read your future?"

Trying to keep my eyes on the kids, I responded, "No thanks – but you already knew that, didn't you?"

Several seconds later I noticed my wife staring at me. "What?" I asked.

She replied, "I can't believe you just said that."

Suddenly we spotted the restaurant, and I was off the hook.

* * *

We seem to spend a lot of time these days trying to find places. It could be the house of a new friend, a particular store, or the address of a soccer field in another town. In the case of the latter, with D1, D2 and D3 on three separate travel soccer teams and the matches/tournaments getting farther away, we often find ourselves turning to MapQuest for help.

I am one of those people who was not only born with a good sense of direction, but also with an ability to almost always keep my orientation, even on a cloudy day. Having grown up in New Jersey, I also have a very good sense of where most places are in relation to the main roads and key landmarks. All in all, it's pretty hard for me to get lost in the daylight – just show me the destination on a map, and let's go.

Notwithstanding the above, if I do get lost, I *really* get lost, and I don't pretend otherwise. As soon as I realize it, I have no problem stopping and asking for help. I am given to understand that this is not a typical male trait, so perhaps I am directionally in better touch with my feminine side.

My wife, on the other hand, does not have a good sense of direction at all. Maps do not help her very much. Give her an accurate set of printed directions, and she can follow them diligently to a successful

---

arrival at the desired destination. The problems she faces, however, are:

- Riding with several noisy kids in the car can create difficulty in concentrating on directions.
- MapQuest is not always exactly correct.
- While finding one's way to the destination may be accomplished with some degree of success, finding one's way home requires following the directions in reverse. Remembering to turn the opposite way - especially out of the parking lot - can be particularly tricky. (*Note: for some reason, printing out a second set of MapQuest directions from the destination to the origin seems not to be a viable option.*)

And so, my wife often finds herself in some part of New Jersey in a situation where she is less than entirely certain of her location with reference to her intended route. In other words, she gets lost a lot! At such times, she does not hesitate to reach out for help either. Apparently she is in full communication with her feminine side as well. It is the way in which she asks for help that can test her sanity and mine. Consider the following:

The Scene: My cell phone buzzes in my pocket. I answer it.

My Beloved Wife: "Where am I?"

Her Equally Loving Husband: "Hi, Honey."

Wife: "I'm lost!"

Husband: "I'm standing in Miami International Airport waiting to go through security – where are you?"

Wife: "I don't know. Help me."

Husband: "How can I help you if I don't know where you are? You are going to have to give me more to go on than that."

Wife: "I'm somewhere in South Jersey trying to find my way back from D2's soccer game."

Husband: "Can you be a little more specific? A town name, a route number, anything."

Wife: "These MapQuest directions are wrong."

Husband: "Didn't you say you are on your way home?"

Wife: "Yes"

Husband: "How wrong could they be? They were good enough to get you there."

Unfortunately the brilliance of this insight is lost in the moment.

Wife: "Come on, your children are cranky, we are all hungry, and I need help here."

Uh oh, did anyone else pick up on the phrase "your children?"

Husband: "How can I help you when you haven't told me where you are? Did I mention that I am in MIAMI?"

Wife: "I'm passing a Home Depot and a Target."

Husband: "OK, that narrows it down to about 400 locations in New Jersey. Can you give me anything more?"

Wife: "I see a sign that says '130 South'."

Husband: "You are in South Jersey trying to get home – why are you going South?"

Wife: "I don't know – just tell me where to go."

Husband: "Well, if you keep driving south for the next 22 hours you can pick me up here in Miami."

Wife: "That's not even close to funny!"

Husband: "Come on, that was at least worth a chuckle. "

Silence – I guess it wasn't funny.

Husband: "Look, here's what you do – find a place to turn around, follow that road until you hit Route 1, go north to New Brunswick, and you should be able to get home from there."

Forty minutes later, I'm still waiting for my flight when the cell phone buzzes again.

Wife: "I'm home. I am <u>never</u> doing this again."

I don't take the bait. Directionally challenged though she may be, my wife is apparently in touch with her masculine side, as she will never admit that she is not equal to a challenge. And so, next week I can expect a call while driving home from work saying, "Honey, I think I'm somewhere in Westfield. How do I get home, and DON'T LAUGH!"

* * *

I was thinking perhaps in our next car we should get one of those GPS computers. It seems fairly straightforward. Just key in the address, and then the unit tells you "Turn left, turn right, go straight."

However, I recently overheard a conversation between my wife's mom and uncle. Despite the fact that he was riding in her car with fully equipped GPS, he had to call from his cell phone to ask her for directions – on how to use the GPS!

I think I would rather stick to giving turn-by-turn instructions from Miami.

* * *

Autor's Note: The bit about the GPS was added almost as an afterthought. I was therefore quite surprised when all of the responses from the readers dealt with the GPS rather than getting lost. As a result, I changed my mind and presented The Queen with a brand new Garmin GPS as a holiday gift.

See the Appendix for a sample of the GPS blog posts.

32. Interview with the Gardener

November/December, Year 3

As Year 3 draws to a close, your faithful Gardener recently sat down for a chat with Barbara Walters, and the transcript of the interview appears below.

* * *

Announcer: "Due to the Hollywood script writers' strike, tonight's episode of *Grey's Anatomy* will not be seen. Instead, we bring you this Barbara Walters Special, followed by endless reruns of *The Practice*."

Music... Barbara Walters is sitting in a chair facing a very dashing mid-40's man wearing an open collared shirt. The executive producer rises to his feet and leaves the room. I enter and sit down.

Barbara Walters (BW): "Welcome to the ABC Barbara Walters Special. I'm Barbara Walters, and tonight we are going to spend some time with The Gardener. Let's get right to it. Mr. Gardener, are your daughters really named D1-D4?"

Uh oh, this interview could be a challenge. Did she spend all night thinking up that one?

The Gardener (TG): "No, they have real names. However, I don't expect my readers to remember the birth order, and it's as much about the observations as it is about the kids, anyway."

BW: "Did everything in the Postcards really happen?"

TG: "There are three kinds of Postcards. Some of them are completely whimsical and made up (such as the various Valentine's Day editions – *Romeo and Juliet* et al.) Some are musings about what <u>might</u> happen in the future, such as when my daughters get their drivers licenses or start wearing makeup. In these I try to at least reflect the personalities of the women in my life. Both of the first two types should be pretty obvious. The third are factual. In a factual Postcard, if I put quotes around what someone said it is as close as possible to what I remember, subject to cleanup for grammar. The only creative license I will take is sometimes I will combine multiple events/conversations for brevity."

BW: "If you were a tree, what kind of tree would you be?"

TG: "I beg your pardon?" *Didn't she ask this of Katherine Hepburn?*

BW: "What is the most challenging part about living with five women?"

TG: "Top of the list is getting into the bathroom.

Everything else is a distant second."

BW: "Will there be more Postcards about this subject?"

TG: "You can count on it."

BW: "Ever wish you had sons?"

TG: "Aside from the bathroom part, no. The girls like soccer, skiing, ice hockey, baseball, NASCAR, and football, to name a few. Just last weekend we were watching the Giants-Eagles football game on TV. The Giants receiver caught a pass and broke free in the secondary. Suddenly D2 yelled, 'HE COULD...GO...ALL...THE...WAY!' What more do I need than my own little version of Chris Berman in the house? Seriously though, after a triplet pregnancy and then one more, just having four healthy children is more than enough of a blessing for anyone – how many of which gender just doesn't matter."

BW: "What gave you the idea to start writing these Postcards in the first place?"

TG: "It was kind of an accident. One day the kids were scrambling around the house getting ready to go to worship service, and the scene was so comical that I had to write it down. I sent it to a handful of people as a lark, and the reaction was so positive that I figured I would do a few more. The readership just kept growing, eventually reaching about nine different countries around the world."

BW: "Did anyone in particular inspire you from an artistic standpoint?"

TG: "I have always enjoyed reading MarkTwain and Isaac Asimov. In addition to being novelists, both men were prolific essayists. The ability to be simultaneously insightful, succinct, and clever in the choice of words is a talent I admire."

BW: "Anyone inspire you who is still alive?"

TG: "I love the stand-up comedy of Billy Crystal, Bill Cosby, Ray Romano, Jerry Seinfeld, etc. These guys can be incredibly funny without being crude. There's nothing wrong with being a bit risqué, but the trick is to do so in a way that is suggestive rather than offensive."

BW: "When do you find time to write?"

TG: "I travel a lot internationally. When I get tired of working or reading on a long flight, I just sit back, close my eyes, and think of the five women in my life. Or I will suddenly wake up in the middle of the night with an idea and run to the computer. Sometimes I just sit down with my daughters, ask them questions, and take notes. Unfortunately, however, they are starting to get wise to this technique – I may need to start wearing one of those police body wires to record my conversations with them."

BW: "What does your wife think of all this?"

TG: "My wife, The Queen, is my primary editor, the source of much of my material, and the judge of whether the final result is good enough to send out. I hand her a draft and walk into the next room. If I can hear her laughing, I know it's a keeper."

BW: "And your daughters?"

TG: "If the Postcard is about them, I always give the girls a preview to make sure I'm not upsetting anyone – they usually find it very funny."

BW: "What do you imagine other women think when they read your Postcards?"

TG: "I think I probably validate their choice in a mate. They are particularly happy they didn't marry someone with my warped sense of humor."

BW: "Do you get any unexpected reactions from the readers?"

TG: "Well, American expressions don't always travel. One time I mentioned that my kids have many 'stuffed animals', and one of my Norwegian readers thought I was talking about taxidermy instead of plush toys."

BW: "Any good stories from the readers?"

TG: "Yes, and some of the Postcards generate rather unexpected responses. The blog posts on Laundry, Physics and Theology put me in stitches, as did their ruminations on their GPS devices (see Appendix)."

BW: "Wow, some of your readers are very clever. Now tell us, when is your book coming out?"

TG: "It's in the works. Why, do you know a good literary agent?"

BW: "No, I don't even know what kind of tree I would be. Well, there you have it, our interview with The Gardener. Don't forget to tune in for your local news at 11:00."

Epilogue

Dear Reader,

Thank you for joining me on this brief journey. If three years seem to have passed quickly in these pages, to me they have disappeared in the blink of an eye. I am grateful for whatever moved me to start writing it down.

As this narrative draws to a close, the triplets have just turned 11, and my daughters are starting to show hints of the women they will become. Amazing! D4 still looks like a child most of the time, especially when she is sleeping, but the presence of three older sisters has an accelerating effect.

What will the next years bring? I don't really know. But if the last three years are any indication, it will be an interesting ride in the Garden of Estrogen.

A preview of Book 2 of the Garden of Estrogen Series appears following the Appendix.

All the Best,

Your Faithful Gardener

APPENDIX - THE READERS TAKE OVER

As mentioned in Chapters 11 and 32, some of my readers can be extremely funny in their own right. Here is a sample of some of the most clever blog responses.

Laundry, Physics and Theology -
A Reprise

The Postcard on Laundry, Physics and Theology generated a surprising combination of highly intellectual and down to earth responses. Note in particular the very last one.

* * *

A male reader blogged:

> I am also the child of a Physics Professor, and I am married to an Elementary School teacher. It would seem that I am equally qualified, perhaps more so, to provide <u>irrefutable</u> evidence that refutes your <u>irrefutable</u> evidence!
>
> By your own assertion, white light is the presence of all colors and black is the absence of light. If we agree on this, then we are left with several possible alternative conclusions.
>
> • Could the black towel be gray simply because some or all of your white laundry may be dyed white, and blended with the blackness to create gray?

- Could the now gray towels be in a state of perpetual grayness due to the extraordinary mass of laundry produced daily by five women and one man ... perhaps enough mass to create a miniature black hole inside your house ... the light may be bent towards the mass in such a way as to create a subtle, less black look ... perhaps a distortion of the truth that the towels may still truly be black?

- Could the purported Fortunoff pre-wash be nothing more than a ruse? A splash of browns and blues, covering a deep non-lustrous gray tone, all designed to disappear over time and make visible the very gray that you observed?

In fact, if you were an artist, the only conclusion that you could have drawn would have been that not all issues are truly <u>black</u> or <u>white</u> ... they are oftentimes quite <u>gray</u>. Just open and close the washing machine cover several thousand times per second, for a millennia or two ... the clothes will appear both black and white simultaneously ... or for the casual observer, gray!

This blogger then proceeded to launch into an explanation of Einstein's theory of relativity, and how clothing in motion appears to a stationary observer (complete with links to the Stanford University Physics Dept), but you get the general idea.

Another male reader responded:

Being partially color-blind, I find this all quite amusing. Regarding your two experiments:

- I could not successfully perform the 1st experiment - I'd probably color both pieces either red or green, and I wouldn't know the difference. If I spun them, they'd be what you would call purple or aqua-blue, but I am sure I would see "white."

- As to the 2nd experiment - I would see nothing and so would all of you. As a matter of physics I'd argue that once you turn the light out there is nothing to see. Light conveys color as a particle wavelength. The receptors in your eyes receive the electro magnetic radiation (light) and translate it into a color. The receptors in my eyes are not attuned to the wavelengths of what you call red and green. So I see them considerably differently. But it doesn't matter since in a dark room (i.e., no light of any color bouncing around) you can not see anything. And neither would I.

This blogger went on to quote Rogers and Hammerstein:

Remember what Julie Andrews sang in the Sound of Music – "Nothing bounces off of nothing, nothing ever could." Or was it "Nothing comes from nothing…"

Yet another male quoted Cole Porter:

"Remember - it's always darkest…just before they turn on the lights."

- Moonface Martin in *Anything Goes*

And finally, a female reader weighed in:

I can't believe you guys have time to think about, research, and write scholarly blogs about laundry and theology. I'm sure your wives have many

---

things on their lists for you to do if you have that kind of free time!

Author's Note: The Queen says, "Amen to that!"

Directions - GPS Thoughts

Apparently some people have a love-hate relationship with their GPS. Here are three very funny observations from my readers.

* * *

A reader from Pennsylvania blogs:

> My wife has a cell phone that contains, among many other things, a GPS. It is affixed to the holder on the dashboard before the key is put in the ignition...even when she is going to the grocery store, which hasn't moved since it was first built and is still only three right-hand turns and less than a mile from our house.

And another from Virginia:

> We actually just got a car with a NAV system. Mind you, we didn't want one. My husband and I thought it would expedite the destruction of the brain cells that we use to get to/figure out where we need to go. But all of the cars on the lot had one, so our disinterest in the NAV system became part of our negotiations to bring down the price of the car.

Anyway, as you might expect two engineers would, we are really enjoying it. We find ourselves programming familiar places just for the fun of it and for the satisfaction of hearing a voice confirm that we know where we are going.

We are not, however, ready to let our son use it. It was somewhat of an eye opener to us that after 17 years of driving in a car around our neighborhood, he got lost coming home from the movie theater. We blame that on years of looking at TVs or listening to iPods with eyes closed instead of looking out the window while in the car. We have decided that if we let our son depend on a NAV system now, he would never be able to find his way around on his own!

And finally, one from Singapore:

If you're planning on getting a GPS for the car, why not buy a fun foreign version? I'll explain...

My husband and I are very anti-GPS, for different reasons. He can find his way out of any place blindfolded; I cannot find my way out of my bathroom unaided, but I don't like machinery telling me what to do (question of pride!)

We recently went to rural Japan for a holiday, though, and the rental car automatically came with a GPS. Once we realised that this was a GOOD thing - if only because we couldn't read the road signs in Japanese - we began to enjoy the particular traits of a Japanese GPS.

The lady who directs you is not just some discombobulated voice; she's actually pictured in cutesy "manga" on the screen, and she comes and goes every time she needs to tell you something (which is rather often.) What's more, as Japanese politesse requires, she bows upon entering, bows upon speaking, bows upon speaking more, bows even more cutely and then does a flippant little wave upon leaving the screen. In fact, with all that infectious bowing going on, it was amazing we could even keep our eyes on the road! Also, she speaks in the most syrupy sweet voice...hmmmm...and it's NONSTOP.

The net result is that, after 10 days in Hokkaido I've returned to Singapore, but still every left or right turn inspires me to bow, wave, flip and enunciate in treacly tones, "Suminasem, Hidariho Ko-ones, Mihigo Ko-ones, Ari-igato-oo..."

I mean, people are beginning to stare oddly......

So, maybe you can get the Japanese version of GPS for New Jersey and transform the Staffin girls into a bowing quintet?

As for me, let's see, where's that bathroom door again...Hidariho Ko-ones?

PREVIEW: THE GARDENER RETURNS

The following is an excerpt from Book 2 of The Garden of Estrogen Series. As of this printing it is still a work in progress – as are my children. We'll all just have to wait to see how it turns out.

Cows and County Fairs

Sometime in Year 4

My children have all taken a liking to cows. Real live cows: MOOO, and all that. For the last two years D1 has been a member of the 4-H Dairy Club, helping to care for a female Holstein at a local farm. She wants to be a dairy farmer when she grows up, but to round out her bovine education, this year she has added a yearling female Hereford (breeder beef cow). D2 and D3 have also taken on female Hereford beef breeder calves, and D4 may start showing dairy cows as early as this summer as well. As for The Queen and me, this puts us knee deep in – well, you can fill in the blank.

Spending so much time hanging around a farm, I am worried that my children might be getting the wrong ideas about gender. I decide to take preemptive action:

Father *(approaching D1 as she is studying)*: "Hey, D1, you know how on the farm if a female is born, the cow is kept, but if a male is born, they turn it into a steer and sell it for steak?"

D1 (*wondering where this is going*): "Yes?"

The Queen, busy preparing dinner, peeks around the corner. She is curious as well.

Father: "You realize it works differently if you ever have a son."

D1: "Daaaaad!"

The Queen bursts out laughing.

* * *

A large portion of our summer activities revolve around various county fairs, courtesy of our afore-mentioned would-be dairy farmer and her fellow bovine-loving siblings. During a break from the cow show at one such fair, the whole family took a walk through the myriad of booths and ultimately stopped for a snack. The girls went about the task of demolishing an order of "fried Oreo's," while I sat at the end of the picnic table engaged in one of my favorite pastimes – observing the interaction between human males and females.

One such couple in their 20's were engaged in a spirited conversation. Evidently they had become separated in the crowd, and it took some time to reunite, to their mutual frustration.

I heard the man say, "Don't you know how they do it in the military? If you get lost, you sit down, and eventually you will be found."

This seemed logical to me, until I heard the reply from his female companion. "And what if we both get lost? Then we'll just be sitting there like idiots forever. What good is that?"

At that point one of my girls stood up from the table covered in powdered sugar, ending my observation. As a result, I have no idea if the poor fellow had a clever comeback. However, given the proximity of all those cows, I think the fellow's best course of action would be to say nothing, lest his female companion try to sell him for steak as well.

Acknowledgements

Although it was not my intent to write a book when I sent out the first few Postcards, when I finally decided to do so, I discovered what an undertaking it is. Many people are required to successfully bring a project like this to fruition – some by tangible contributions, others by the valuable suggestions they offer, and still others by friendship, love and moral support.

Many thanks to my illustrator Darlene Cordero, and my publisher Dog Ear Publishing, LLC, for their professional help in transforming a manuscript into a book.

And heartfelt gratitude to the following people:

- Longtime friend Steve Shapiro, whose book, *Goal Free Living*, demonstrated that setting a direction is far more important than setting a destination.
- Gaylene Pepe, for managing to convince an aspiring engineer to get creative.
- Pastor Jeff Gibelius, for providing moral support and periodic (though sometimes unintentional) theological input, and Rabbi Alfred Landsberg,

whose ability to combine wit and wisdom inspired much of the biblical humor in this book.

- Maria and Peter Lagios, and Terry and Denis Bovin, for all the kind feedback.
- Chris Kerr, Dale Hansen and Mark Dransfield for their input in the final stages before production.
- Ramsey El-Fakir, Jill Staffin, Liz Dransfield, Susan Metz, Lori Traweek, Nicholas Wolfson, Kum Kum Seth, Mark Nassi, Jodi Levine, Louis Cavaliere, Chris Sheraden, Linda Lacke and Mark Holford for their insightful comments and observations.
- All the readers of my monthly newsletter, from the USA to Denmark to Singapore and many places in between.
- Martha Haldopoulos (Queen Mother and my biggest fan), Peter Haldopoulos (Grand Patriarch of the Garden).
- My mom, Anne, from whom I have inherited a love of expression through the written word, and her mom, Claire Schneider, who became one of the original self publishers decades ago by setting up her own company.
- My sister Linda, and brother Eric, whose encouragement and support helped make this book a reality.
- My daughters, for filling the days with laughter and tolerating this intrusion into their formative years.

And finally, Christiana Staffin, my beloved Queen of the Garden of Estrogen: primary editor, confidant, co-conspirator, and best friend.

Don Staffin

A New Jersey resident who lives with his wife and four daughters, Don Staffin has been writing a monthly newsletter called *Postcards from the Garden of Estrogen* since 2004. He is a recognized leader in the field of international marine e-commerce, and an accomplished public speaker. He holds bachelors and masters degrees in engineering and an MBA, all from Cornell University.

Printed in the United States
148899LV00001B/2/P